ICONIC
PEOPLE OF COLOUR

ELIZABETH AJAO

Illustrations by Phil Shaw

summersdale

ICONIC PEOPLE OF COLOUR

Copyright © Summersdale Publishers Ltd, 2022

Illustrations by Phil Shaw

An Hachette UK Company
www.hachette.co.uk

Summersdale Publishers Ltd
Part of Octopus Publishing Group Limited
Carmelite House
50 Victoria Embankment
LONDON
EC4Y 0DZ
UK

www.summersdale.com

Printed and bound in Poland

ISBN: 978-1-78783-977-9

Substantial discounts on bulk quantities of Summersdale books are available to corporations, professional associations and other organizations. For details contact general enquiries: telephone: +44 (0) 1243 771107 or email: enquiries@summersdale.com.

CONTENTS

For James, without whom I could not have written this book, and for every person who needs a sprinkle of inspiration

INTRODUCTION

Oh, hello! By picking up this book, you have taken the first step in educating yourself further on the incredible people of colour (POC) who have shaped our world. Although you've shown an interest in striving for change, ugly stereotypes about POC have sadly permeated the workplaces, schools and streets of our planet for centuries.

Despite this, whether it's in the science labs, the charts, on the silver screen or even in the White House, we have proven that the prejudice we've faced is just a load of rubbish.

This book contains profiles of 38 passionate, powerful and pretty darn impressive POC that you *need* to know about. In their own way, they've each defied expectations and made history in the process. Keep this with you and read it whenever you need a reminder of what *any* human being can accomplish, even when extra hurdles are thrown in their way!

ALEXANDRIA OCASIO-CORTEZ

13/10/1989—PRESENT

HER SUPERPOWERS:

She's not just Any Outstanding Character...
She's not just Any Ordinary Congresswoman...
She's AOC: Alexandria Ocasio-Cortez, the
youngest woman ever to serve in US Congress.

HER INCREDIBLE STORY

AOC is the daughter of Puerto-Rican parents, Blanca and Sergio Ocasio-Roman. She was raised in the Bronx until she was five. Then, thanks to her father's success as an architect, the family moved to one of New York's more swanky counties, Westchester.

After leaving Yorktown High School in 2007, AOC went to Boston University to major in economics and international relations. A double degree! However, tragedy struck in 2008 when her beloved father passed away from lung cancer. The family found themselves with financial difficulties, and Blanca's job as a housekeeper wasn't enough to keep the OCs afloat. They sold their home and headed to Florida.

Upon finishing college, Alexandria moved back to the Bronx. Older and wiser, she quickly noticed that the residents of Westchester had more opportunities available to them than the people she was meeting in the Bronx, and just like that (snap your fingers, please), she knew she had to create some *serious* change.

Working as an intern for US Senator Ted Kennedy during college prepared AOC for her job as an organizer for Bernie Sanders' campaign in the 2016 Primary Election. When the election was over, she travelled all around America, where she spoke to working class people who were struggling to cope after disasters within their community. Before the trip, AOC had thought that the only way to get somewhere in politics was to be rich, popular and powerful. However, seeing these communities pull together to solve their problems made her remember what politics was all about: making positive change!

Just one day after her trip, AOC got the phone call that changed everything. Brand New Congress (a committee formed by people who'd worked for Bernie Sanders in 2016) was searching for progressive candidates, and Alexandria was one of them.

Despite her previous concerns that her financial situation might limit her political success, AOC ran her campaign from behind the taco bar where she was a waitress.

After beating Joe Crowley in the 2018 mid-terms (much to the horror of Republicans across America), AOC managed to win the Reform Party primary election without campaigning. Voters simply wrote her name on the ballot slips. Given that she hadn't actually run, she chose not to accept the nomination.

In the next round of campaigns for the general election, she was endorsed by Bernie Sanders and even Barack Obama! AOC smashed it, winning a whopping 78 per cent of the vote.

Not only is she the youngest woman to serve in US Congress, she is also one of the most influential politicians ever to have graced America. She has proven to young women and POC *everywhere* that no matter where or what you come from, you can be as successful as you want to if you try. AOC, please be the next president? You'd absolutely slay.

AMAZING FACTS AND ACHIEVEMENTS

→ AOC launched her own publishing firm, Brook Avenue Press, when she was 22.

→ AOC has an asteroid named after her, called Asteroid 23238 Ocasio-Cortez! It was a prize for coming second place in a science fair in high school.

→ Several quotes have been misattributed to her, including, "I have a very good brain and I've said lots of things." Any guesses as to who *actually* said that?

→ After her victory against Joe Crowley, Merriam-Webster announced that searches for "socialism" on their online dictionary rose by a gigantic 1,500 per cent!

→ Between 25 February and 7 April 2019, Fox News/Fox Business mentioned AOC's name around 75 times PER DAY.

"I AM EXPERIENCED ENOUGH TO DO THIS. I AM KNOWLEDGEABLE ENOUGH TO DO THIS. I AM PREPARED ENOUGH TO DO THIS. I AM MATURE ENOUGH TO DO THIS. I AM BRAVE ENOUGH TO DO THIS."

BARACK OBAMA

09/08/1961—PRESENT

HIS SUPERPOWERS:

They say not all heroes wear capes and it's true – the former US president Barack Obama wears a suit, a tie and one of his four identical pairs of black, size 11 shoes.

HIS INCREDIBLE STORY

Barack Hussein Obama II was born in Hawaii to Ann Dunham from Kansas and Barack Obama Sr from Kenya. When Barack was just two years old, his father left Honolulu for Harvard University. Little did this tiny tot know that he'd only see his father once more, for his parents divorced just a year later and his father moved back to Kenya, where he would pass away in a car accident in 1982. His mother remarried soon after the divorce, and the family moved to Indonesia when Barack was six.

When Barack was just ten, he moved back to Hawaii, where he lived with his grandparents or his mother; sometimes she was away, working on her PhD. After divorcing her second husband, Barack's mother struggled financially, but this didn't stop her from giving her son the best life she could. By the time he was 18, Barack was graduating from Punahou School, a very chic school in Honolulu.

He started studying at Occidental College, LA, and after two years transferred to Columbia, where he undertook his bachelor's degree in political science. Following a DMC (deep, meaningful conversation) with his teachers, Barack started pushing himself; he got his head down and began reading dense, complicated works by Shakespeare and Nietzsche. After a short time as a writer and editor in Manhattan, he moved to Chicago and took a job as a community organizer in the poorer Far South Side of the Windy City. Not long after that, he started studying at Harvard University's law school. You might notice a theme, here, because Obama soon became the first African American president of the esteemed *Harvard Law Review*. He graduated *magna cum laude* and then became an associate at a Chicago law firm, where he met a phenomenal woman, Michelle Robinson – I'm sure you already know where this is going... The pair were married in 1992, and they had two beautiful daughters, Sasha and Malia.

Let's skip through the complex ins and outs of US politics and fast-forward to 2008. Democrat candidate Barack Hussein Obama had just been elected the 44th President of the United States of America. His running mate was Joe Biden (who would go on to become US president himself!). Forever overachieving, not only was Obama the first Black president of the US, he also got the most votes out of *any* president, ever! Legend.

When he was taking office, America was in financial turmoil, grappling with climate change and war. Did that stop him from absolutely slaying in his role as president? Heck, no. He turned the economy around; he reformed the US healthcare system with "Obamacare"; he steered America towards a more eco-conscious future, and all the while he was proving to millions of POC that anything was possible.

AMAZING FACTS AND ACHIEVEMENTS

→ Obama was the first president to be born outside of mainland US, which caused a bit of a stir with Donald Trump, who insisted Obama prove he was really American! Obviously, he was.

→ Barack is the proud author of three books: *Dreams from my Father* (1995), *The Audacity of Hope* (2006) and *Of Thee I Sing: A Letter to My Daughters* (2010).

→ Rounding off Obama's record, he was responsible for "2017's Most Liked Tweet": a photo of him with some children of colour and the beautiful caption, "No one is born hating another person because of the color of his skin or his background or his religion." It got 1.7 million retweets and 4.5 million likes!

"KEEP EXPLORING. KEEP DREAMING. KEEP ASKING WHY. DON'T SETTLE FOR WHAT YOU ALREADY KNOW. NEVER STOP BELIEVING IN THE POWER OF YOUR IDEAS, YOUR IMAGINATION, YOUR HARD WORK TO CHANGE THE WORLD."

BESSIE COLEMAN

26/01/1892—30/04/1926

HER SUPERPOWERS:

Some superheroes are invisible, some can read your mind, but "Brave Bessie" Coleman was the first African American and Native American woman to fly.

HER INCREDIBLE STORY

Bessie was born in Texas to Susan, an African American maid, and George, a Native American sharecropper. This was a subtle, modernized form of slavery: sharecroppers would receive food, tools, shelter and land in exchange for a share of the crops they produced. To escape the ordeal of living as a person of colour in the south, George moved to Oklahoma. Susan decided to keep her family with her in Texas. With George gone, Bessie helped her mother pick cotton to earn money, and she eventually saved enough to attend the Colored Agricultural and Normal University in Oklahoma. Sadly, experiencing more financial prob•lems, Bessie was forced to leave college after just one term.

Bessie moved to Chicago to live with her brothers, who had returned from fighting in World War One. They would taunt her with stories about the women in France who were able to fly magnificent planes, knowing that Bessie was not able to, being a woman of colour. Now, girls don't like being told they can't do something, so naturally, Bessie tried to become a pilot. Her colour and gender meant she wasn't accepted by any US flying schools, so she took French classes to allow her to write an application to a school in France.

It worked! Bessie was accepted to the Caudron Brothers' School of Aviation, and she received her international pilot's licence in 1921. She gave speeches about flying and showed footage of her amazing loop-the-loops and figure-of-eights to crowds of people in churches, theatres and schools to earn a living. The headstrong woman who refused to accept that she couldn't fly would certainly not perform to any segregated audiences or anywhere that discriminated against POC. Word spread of this young, new pilot, and she toured around Europe and the US. Everywhere she went, she encouraged marginalized people to learn how to fly.

The flight shows and teaching paid off, because Bessie's dream came true and she was finally able to buy her own plane. She returned to her home town to perform but refused when she found out that her Black and white audience would be entering through different doorways. Bessie stuck to her guns, and, after kicking up a suitable fuss, performed on the proviso that her audience would all enter through the same door.

Bessie died in 1926 after a fatal accident during a test flight with mechanic William Wills. Bessie is not a particularly well-known woman of colour, but she absolutely should be. Anybody else suddenly feel compelled to take up flying?

AMAZING FACTS AND ACHIEVEMENTS

➔ A street in Florida was renamed "Bessie Coleman Street" in honour of the pilot in 2013.

➔ Bessie was one of 13 children!

➔ Two years after receiving her licence, Bessie was injured in one of her stunt shows – she broke a leg and three ribs! Didn't stop her from bouncing straight back, though.

➔ Since 1931, there has been a tradition of flying over Bessie's grave once a year in memory of this amazing woman.

➔ Bessie was offered a role in a movie called *Shadows and Sunshine*, but she rejected the part when she discovered her character would appear in stereotypically "Black" tattered clothes, with a walking stick and backpack.

➔ Her absolute dream was to own a flying school for young women and POC, but she died before she was able to. In 1977, a group of female African American pilots formed the Bessie Coleman Aviators Club.

"TELL THEM THAT AS SOON AS I CAN WALK, I'M GOING TO FLY!"

BUFFY SAINTE-MARIE

c.20/02/1941—PRESENT

HER SUPERPOWERS:

This Buffy might not slay vampires, but she has definitely slayed at making music with a message.

HER INCREDIBLE STORY

Born in the Cree, one of the largest First Nations (groups of Indigenous peoples) in Canada, Buffy Sainte-Marie is nothing short of an absolute icon.

Buffy's mother passed away when she was just a baby, so she was adopted by Albert and Winifred Sainte-Marie from Massachusetts. When she was a toddler, she'd bash pots and pans, entranced by the different noises each one made. At three, she moved onto bashing the piano instead, refusing to stop until it made a sound that she liked. It wasn't until she was 16 that she first picked up a guitar, but she fell in love with it straight away. She retuned the strings in countless ways, meaning that all of her music was totally unique.

In her early twenties, Buffy started playing at folk music festivals and First Nations reservations around the US. She frequently performed in coffee houses, and often found herself in the company of up-and-coming musicians: think Leonard Cohen, Joni Mitchell and Neil Young! Buffy's career got a big boost when Bob Dylan heard her sing in Greenwich Village and begged her to perform at Gaslight, a popular hangout for the folk community.

In 1963, Buffy's entire career started to crumble when she developed bronchial pneumonia: an illness which nearly destroyed her voice for good. She then became addicted to painkillers, and, as a sort of self-therapy, wrote the song "Cod'ine", which has since been covered by several famous folkies, including Courtney Love. Later that year, a critic from *The New York Times* gave Buffy an amazing review, which spun her toward a contract with Vanguard Records, with whom she released her first album a year later, called *It's My Way!*

This was the first of over 15 albums, all full of music with a message: be it the treatment of Native Americans, pacifism or love. In 1976, the year she gave birth to her child, Buffy began a 15-year break from recording. Around this time, she was starting to lose popularity because she had become so politically vocal. Her outspoken attitude to the causes she cared about (such as the anti-Vietnam War movement and the American Indian Movement) resulted in her being banished from a large portion of mainstream radio.

Buffy has always been immensely passionate about education for and about the Native American community. She founded the Nihewan Foundation for Native American Education in 1969, and even became a star of *Sesame Street*, where she was able to educate younger children about Native American culture. Buffy is still singing and writing songs that tell us what we need to hear, and long may she continue!

AMAZING FACTS AND ACHIEVEMENTS

➜ Buffy's 2015 album, *Power in the Blood*, received the 2015 Polaris Music Prize for the best Canadian album.

→ She thinks of her song "Universal Soldier" as more like journalism than music.

→ Although 2020 was a difficult year for everyone thanks to that pesky pandemic, one great thing that came out of it was Buffy's children's book, *Hey Little Rockabye: A Lullaby for Pet Adoption*.

→ Buffy has two degrees, one in teaching and another in oriental philosophy, *and* she graduated in the top ten in her class.

→ Buffy likes to do unusual things that nobody else in the industry does: she sang a song in Hindi (at the time, it wasn't a mainstream language in the US), and has often used an instrument called a mouth bow.

→ In 1975, she married Sheldon Wolfchild, and they had a son, Dakota "Cody" Starblanket Wolfchild a year later.

"TAKE A BUNCH OF LITTLE KIDS TO THE BEACH AND THEY ALL MAKE ART... THEY'LL USE THEIR IMAGINATIONS, MAKE DRAMA... MAKE PICTURES IN THE SAND, THEY'LL MAKE UP SONGS THAT NO ONE'S EVER HEARD BEFORE."

CHADWICK BOSEMAN

29/11/1976—28/08/2020

HIS SUPERPOWERS:

Chadwick Boseman was a superhero both on and off the screen who will never be forgotten.

HIS INCREDIBLE STORY

Chadwick Boseman was one of the most influential actors of his generation, rising to fame after portraying baseball player Jackie Robinson in 42. He was the first Black actor to star in the lead role of a Marvel movie, and following this he was named one of *TIME* magazine's 100 most influential people.

Born and raised in South Carolina, as a child, Chadwick frequently experienced racial abuse at school. Despite the fact that his area had been desegregated a few years before his birth, he still walked past Confederate flags on his way to school and once recalled how he had to avoid a certain route after being alerted that he was heading straight toward a Ku Klux Klan rally.

After graduating from high school, he studied directing at Howard University, Washington DC. Howard University is renowned for its large percentage of Black students, where over 86 per cent of the student body are POC. Fun fact: one student at college with Chadwick was Ta-Nehisi Coates, who ended up writing some of the *Black Panther* comics. During this time, Chadwick and some of his classmates were selected to go to Oxford for a summer course, but it came at a cost that he just couldn't afford. Their teacher appealed to some well-known actors for funding, and the actor who helped Chadwick was none other than Denzel Washington!

When he wasn't studying, Chadwick spent his downtime playing basketball. However, when one of his teammates was murdered, he transformed his anger into art and created his first play, *Crossroads*. This wasn't the only amazing thing that came out of his time at Howard; he was also given an honorary degree and was invited back to give an inspirational speech about the power of fighting for the life you deserve. He definitely did uni right!

While we know him best as an actor, Chadwick's heart (and degree) lay behind the scenes. He directed two short films, produced four movies and wrote four plays! From *All My Children* to *CSI: NY*, Chadwick starred in some pretty iconic TV shows. However, it was his role as superhero Black Panther in three Marvel Cinematic Universe films that brought him mainstream media attention. Despite this attention, Chadwick managed to keep some things private: his secret marriage to his girlfriend of five years, singer Taylor Simone Ledward, and his battle with colon cancer. He continued to act until he passed away in August 2020, and his critically acclaimed final film, *Ma Rainey's Black Bottom*, was released in November of that year.

AMAZING FACTS AND ACHIEVEMENTS

→ When he was a child, Chadwick's dream was to become an architect. Is there no end to this guy's talent?

→ In *Gods of Egypt*, Chadwick was shocked that he was the only Black cast member to play one of the Egyptian gods, but still took the part so there was at least *some* representation of POC in the movie.

→ His costume in *Captain America: Civil War* was far too tight – so much so that he struggled to breathe! They managed to get it just right in time for *Black Panther*, though.

→ Shortly after his death, a petition to replace a South Carolina Confederate monument with a statue of Chadwick surpassed its goal of 15,000 signatures, getting 50,000 in under a week.

→ At the beginning of the COVID-19 pandemic, he donated $4.2 million worth of PPE to support hospitals in Black communities.

"I FEEL THAT I'M LIVING MY PURPOSE. BUT THE THING ABOUT PURPOSE IS THAT IT UNFOLDS TO YOU MORE AND MORE EVERY DAY."

FLORENCE PRICE

9/4/1887—3/6/1953

HER SUPERPOWERS:

Single mum of two, virtuoso pianist and champion of bringing Black music into the 20th century – is there anything Florence Price couldn't do?

HER INCREDIBLE STORY

Classical music is known for being made by and for white men, so how did a Black woman come along and smash tradition to pieces?

Florence was born in Little Rock, the capital of Arkansas. Her mother taught all three of her children piano and noticed Florence's musical talent from a young age. Florence gave her first performance at just four years old and published some of her compositions before finishing high school! Florence graduated with honours in piano and organ from the New England Conservatory of Music, and within four years of her graduation she was appointed head of music at Clark Atlanta University.

During the 1920s, Florence won awards for some of her brilliant art songs. One of these, a song titled "To My Little Son", was an ode to her son who tragically died before she gave birth to him.

In 1931, Florence and her husband divorced. Florence took any work she could to provide for her children, including composing radio jingles and playing organ for silent films. A year later, Florence and her housemate, Margaret Bonds, entered the prestigious Wanamaker Foundation Awards. Margaret took first place in the song category, and Florence took first prize in the symphonic works category for her symphony in E minor, as well as taking third prize for her piano sonata – you go girl!

Yes, there was a $500 cash prize, but that wasn't what Florence was most excited about... Her work was to be performed by the Chicago Symphony Orchestra, meaning that she would be the first ever African American woman to have her work performed by a major ensemble.

Following this, Florence became a truly established composer whose work was appreciated by her contemporaries, and throughout the early 1950s, her work started gaining real momentum. She was planning to fly over to Europe to promote her music in 1953, but just before she was due to leave, Florence had a heart attack and passed away.

The attention her work had been gaining seemed to fade into oblivion, as it was scarcely performed in the decades that followed. However, after some of Florence's manuscripts were discovered in an attic, there's been a huge resurgence in appreciation for her music. Musicologists and radio stations around the world have realized that Florence was fabulous and deserved far more credit for her work than she was given.

Finally, Black musicians, and more specifically Black women, were getting the recognition they deserved. Florence, you're an absolute rock star.

AMAZING FACTS AND ACHIEVEMENTS

→ The third movement of Florence's first symphony was performed at BBC's *Last Night of the Proms* in 2021.

→ Professor James Greeson produced a documentary called *The Caged Bird* all about Florence's life and works.

→ Florence wrote her Symphony Number 1 in E Minor while she had a broken foot.

→ She performed at the premiere of her Piano Concerto in One Movement as a soloist with the Chicago Women's Symphony Orchestra in 1934.

→ In 2018, BBC Radio 3 celebrated International Women's Day by giving a broadcast of several of Florence's compositions.

→ Florence was inducted into the American Society of Composers, Authors and Publishers in 1940.

→ Florence was hugely inspired by African American folk songs and would often quote them in her music.

→ Langston Hughes and Florence were fairly close companions and collaborators; he wrote several of the texts for her art songs.

→ Florence composed at least 17 works for orchestra, 14 pieces for choir and over 300 other pieces for solo piano, organ and voice.

FRIDA KAHLO

06/07/1907—13/07/1954

HER SUPERPOWERS:

Despite battling polio, a turbulent relationship and a near-death experience, Frida Kahlo painted her own reality and ran with it.

HER INCREDIBLE STORY

Frida was born in Mexico City to Matilde, a *mestizo* (a person with European and Indigenous American ancestry), and Wilhelm, a German photographer. When Frida was just six, she became infected with polio, an incurable and life-threatening disease. Luckily, she survived, but she couldn't leave her bed for nine months. When she finally did, she found she had lost control of her right leg. Little feminist Frida took up swimming, wrestling and football to help her recover.

In 1922 Frida became one of only a few female students to attend the National Preparatory School, with the dream of becoming a doctor. She met a whole host of people at the school, including artists, communists and other like-minded students, who inspired her to be her unique self. When at school, Frida met a group of pranksters led by Alejandro Gómez, whom she adored. During this time, famous artist Diego Rivera came to the school to create a mural in the dining hall. Frida, Alejandro and their cohort of mischief-makers did all they could to irritate Diego, from covering the stairs in soap to hiding his lunch – they even threw water balloons at him!

In 1925, Frida and Alejandro were together on a bus when the bus collided with a car and one of the metal handrails pierced through Frida's hip. She incurred several injuries, including fractures in her pelvis and her spine, and was hospitalized for weeks. It was when she moved home to recover that her painting career began. Her parents bought her paint and brushes and built her an easel so that she could paint in bed. The result was her first self-portrait, *Self-Portrait in a Velvet Dress*, which she gave to Alejandro as a gift.

Frida had a difficult life, from growing up during the Mexican Revolution, to living with polio and finally her accident, and her canvases are filled with as much emotion as they are paint. Despite working during the dawn of surrealism, Frida seemed to skip straight past it, instead working within realism, taking inspiration from religion and Mexican folklore. If you give her work a quick Google, you'll almost definitely spot a couple of monkeys lurking in the background of her paintings: while they're used as symbols of lust in Mexican tales, Frida used them as little personal guardians to keep her safe!

In 1939, Frida was invited to France to feature in an exhibition, where she became the first 20th-century Mexican artist to have her work purchased by the Louvre, despite selling very few paintings to the general public in her lifetime.

Her artistic career blossomed, and in 1953, Frida presented her first solo exhibition. Despite being bedridden, she refused to miss the opening night – the curators set up a four-poster bed in the middle of the gallery so that she could chat and celebrate with the event's attendees! What a woman.

AMAZING FACTS AND ACHIEVEMENTS

➜ In her 47-year life, Frida produced around 200 paintings, sketches and drawings, 55 of which were self-portraits.

➜ When Frida lived in Paris, she became very good friends with the famous artists Marcel Duchamp and Pablo Picasso.

➜ The 500 Mexican Peso bill has Frida's face on it. On the other side is Diego Rivera's.

➜ In her lifetime, Frida was rarely able to sell her work, although she did take the occasional commission. Nowadays, her works sell for millions, with one self-portrait selling for a whopping $5.62 million in 2006!

➜ Frida has become an icon of Mexican culture, and she wanted it that way... she'd tell people she was born three years after her actual birth so that they'd instantly associate her with the Mexican Revolution, which began in 1910.

➜ Frida's childhood home, named the Blue House due to its cobalt walls, has been turned into a museum, where all of Frida's belongings (and her ashes) can be found exactly as though she still lives there today.

GRACE LEE BOGGS

27/06/1915—05/10/2015

HER SUPERPOWERS:

Few people live to be 100; even fewer dedicate that whole century to helping their community. One of the extraordinary people willing to do just that was Grace Lee Boggs.

HER INCREDIBLE STORY

Born in little Rhode Island, Grace was the proud daughter of Chinese immigrants. Her father was known as "the king of the restaurant businessmen", and she and her five siblings were able to live a comfortable life. After receiving a scholarship to Barnard College (a private women's college) she found herself enthralled by the works of German philosophers Hegel and Kant. She then followed her heart and continued her studies at Bryn Mawr, a liberal women's college, receiving her PhD in 1940 – a feminist from the start!

Due to her ethnicity, Grace struggled to find employment after college and had to accept a very low-paying job at the University of Chicago. During this time, she gravitated towards socialism. It wasn't long before she joined the Workers Party, and in 1941 she took part in the March on Washington; a civil rights march which aimed to pressure the government into providing African Americans with fairer opportunities.

Grace wasn't just campaigning for the equal treatment of African Americans, she was determined to help improve things for *all* POC and women, too. She later found herself in the Johnson-Forest Tendency, another strand of the Workers Party, and spent her time translating letters by Marx and writing articles for the *Correspondence*, the "Johnsonite" publication.

In 1953, Grace moved to Detroit, the epicentre of the Johnson-Forest Tendency. It was in that year that she met and married James Boggs, a Black autoworker and a fellow Johnsonite. The pair passionately fought for the rights of Black Americans and in the autumn of 1963 participated in Martin Luther King Jr's "Great Walk to Freedom".

However, times became tough. Detroit was in the midst of a stark change: factories were closing, and James fell on hard times. Crime was rising and the couple were burgled several times – the thieves even took their front door!

However, nothing was going to stop Grace from trying to change the world. In the 1990s, she attended marches protesting violence against Black women, and she was even part of the development of the Detroit public school curriculum, which included the teaching of conflict resolution in schools. She later launched Detroit Summer, a programme that aimed to bring youth of all races and from all backgrounds into the community, helping them plant gardens and work with other kids. In her final few years, Grace worked with inner-city children to help inspire a new generation of activism in Detroit, and a few years before her death she opened a school.

Grace dedicated her entire life to her community, working unbelievably hard to fight for the equality she knew women and POC deserved. Detroit – and the world – would not be the same without her!

AMAZING FACTS AND ACHIEVEMENTS

➔ Grace is the author of a total of five non-fiction books, all about making positive change – she wrote the last one at the age of 95.

➔ Proud of her Chinese heritage, Grace was also a huge advocate for Detroit Black Power – so much so that people started questioning whether she was actually African American!

➔ Grace first started protesting when, after finding a colony of rats in her community housing, she happened across a group of people who were protesting their poor living conditions and joined in. Gotta start somewhere!

➔ The charter school Grace and her husband founded threw her a 100th birthday party.

➔ In a speech she gave in 1993, Grace talked about how she inherited her passion for politics from her mother, who, despite being unable to read or write, had always wanted to create change.

➔ The Smithsonian Asian Pacific American Center celebrated Grace's 100th birthday by releasing 100 of her best quotes, one for each year of her amazing life.

DR HAYAT SINDI

6/11/1967—PRESENT

HER SUPERPOWERS:

Bachelor's? Check. PhD? Check. First Saudi Arabian woman to get that doctorate from Cambridge? Heck, yeah! Oh, and Dr Hayat Sindi's done a whole lot more than that...

HER INCREDIBLE STORY

Hayat was born in Saudi Arabia, into a world where women's higher education wasn't always valued. However, thanks to her supportive parents and a lot of self-belief, Hayat went into the world knowing that she could do *anything* she wanted. In 1991, she travelled to the UK alone, learned to speak English and got herself some A Levels so that she could apply for university. She tried for several of the world's top universities and was awarded places at King's College London, University of Cambridge, University of Oxford, MIT and Harvard University. Choosing to study at King's, Hayat graduated with a pharmacology degree in 1995, but she wasn't finished with education just yet...

After King's, she went to Newnham College, Cambridge, to embark upon a PhD in biotechnology, which she completed in 2001. While that might seem like a huge feat in itself, it becomes even more impressive when we learn that Hayat was the first woman from *any* of the Arab States of the Persian Gulf (Kuwait, the United Arab Emirates, Qatar, Saudi Arabia, Bahrain, Iraq and Oman) to complete a doctorate in biotechnology, and the first Saudi Arabian woman to be accepted into Cambridge for her field of study. Woah!

Life as a Saudi Arabian woman in academia was tricky, though. Hayat was often shunned for wearing her traditional Muslim headscarf and told to abandon her religious and cultural beliefs. However, Hayat, being the strong woman she is, kindly told those who challenged her to get lost. She kept her headscarf and beliefs, with the full knowledge that what she wore or believed had no hold on her ability as a biotechnologist.

Alongside her work, she is also incredibly vocal about the importance of teaching young women science, technology, engineering and maths (STEM), especially in the Middle East. She has also often highlighted the problem of "brain drain" – the loss of highly trained professionals from certain countries due to emigration.

In 2007, Hayat co-founded Diagnostics For All, for which she invented a device to help diagnose disease quickly, ensuring it was low-cost enough for developing countries. She later founded another organization, the Institute for Imagination Ingenuity, which supports her activism encouraging STEM education for young people. More recently, Hayat has been selected to be on the Shura Council, making her one of the people who advises the Saudi Arabian King on important national issues.

Thanks to people like Hayat, more young women than ever before are working in STEM fields, and the figures are only rising. Her entire life has revolved around bettering the lives of others, through education, science and activism, and we know there's so much more to come!

AMAZING FACTS AND ACHIEVEMENTS

→ In 2012, Saudi royal HRH Prince Khalid bin Faisal Al Saud awarded Hayat the Mekkah Al Mukarramah Prize for scientific innovation.

→ While visiting at Harvard, Hayat produced a documentary promoting science education for young people, alongside four other people. The programme was commissioned by the Executive Office of the President of the US.

→ For her activism encouraging young women to study STEM subjects, Hayat was named a UNESCO Goodwill Ambassador in 2012.

→ *National Geographic* named Hayat an Emerging Explorer in 2011.

→ Hayat made it onto *Newsweek's* 150 Women Who Shake the World list.

"I ALWAYS TREAT MY MIND AS A GARDEN, AND FOCUS ON THE BEAUTIFUL FLOWERS IN IT, DISCARDING ALL THE NEGATIVES, BECAUSE PEOPLE AND THEIR OPINIONS CAN GET TO YOU VERY EASILY."

IEOH MING PEI

26/04/1917—16/05/2019

HIS SUPERPOWERS:

Who needs a Batcave when you can just build a gigantic glass pyramid in the centre of an iconic European landmark? Well, iconic architect Ieoh Ming Pei definitely doesn't...

HIS INCREDIBLE STORY

Ieoh was born to Tsuyee and Lien Kwun in Guangzhou, China. A total mummy's boy from a very young age, Ieoh often joined his mother on meditation retreats. She was a talented flautist, too – I wonder where Ieoh got his artistic talent from?

A successful banker, Tsuyee received a promotion, so the family moved to Shanghai. Despite coming from a Buddhist family, the children attended the Anglican St. John's Middle School. It was intense, to say the least; they were there every single day with just half a day off per month – children in other parts of the world should be thankful for those weekends and half-term holidays!

Around this time, Ieoh was studying outside of school, too; reading the Bible and books by Charles Dickens, he quickly taught himself basic English and became obsessed with Shanghai's Parisian-esque architecture. However, it was also at this time that Lien became unwell with cancer. She sadly passed away when he was just 13, at which time his father became very distant. Completely consumed by work and grief, Tsuyee was unable to look after the children, so they were sent to stay with other family members.

Half a decade later, Ieoh headed to the US: first stop, San Francisco, final destination, the University of Philadelphia. Having watched Hollywood movies set in America, he had high hopes for college life. However, the architecture course was not what he had expected. It taught a traditionalist approach to design, which he had no interest in, so he scrapped architecture and transferred to MIT to study engineering. Imagine being so bright that MIT is your second choice? Still, his lecturers noticed his artistic eye immediately and suggested he return to architecture.

After graduating, he worked as an architect for a real estate brokerage, and in 1949, his first design – a building for Gulf Oil – sprang to life. Soon enough he was the talk of the town, and by 1955 he had steered away from the real estate brokerage he was working for and set up his own firm: I. M. Pei and Associates.

He was asked to design the John F. Kennedy Library, Dallas City Hall and many other brilliant buildings around the world, although it was his project at the Louvre in Paris for which he is probably best known. He put his own stamp on it by erecting a huge glass pyramid right at the centre of the courtyard, and residents and tourists alike have been fascinated by it ever since.

With a legacy of four children, seven grandchildren, five great-grandchildren and nearly 80 projects, I. M. Pei used his 102 years to prove that he wasn't going to let anything hold him back, least of all his skin tone.

AMAZING FACTS AND ACHIEVEMENTS

→ Ieoh was awarded the Pritzker Architecture Prize. The prize money was $100,000, but instead of splashing the cash, Ieoh used it to create a scholarship for aspiring Chinese architects to fund their studies in the US.

→ After getting his bachelor's degree from MIT, Ieoh studied at the Harvard Graduate School of Design, becoming good friends with two well-known Bauhaus architects: Walter Gropius and Marcel Breuer.

→ Ieoh was married to his wife, Eileen Loo, for 70 years before her death in 2014. That's a *lot* of anniversary parties!

→ Not only did Ieoh design nearly 80 buildings in his lifetime, he also received the Presidential Medal of Freedom in 1993.

→ Eileen and Ieoh's three sons all went to Harvard (two of them founded and ran Pei Partnership Architects) and their daughter is a lawyer.

"SUCCESS IS A COLLECTION OF PROBLEMS SOLVED."

JEAN-MICHEL BASQUIAT

22/12/1960—12/08/1988

HIS SUPERPOWERS:

If anyone knew how to go from student who was expelled to world-famous artist who excelled, it was Jean-Michel Basquiat!

HIS INCREDIBLE STORY

Jean-Michel was a Brooklyn baby, born to Puerto-Rican Matilde and Haitian Gérard Basquiat. He was adored by his mother, who often took him to museums and art galleries in Manhattan – she even enrolled him as a member of the Brooklyn Museum of Art when he was little. At the age of four, Jean-Michel was fully literate and showed promise as an artist. He was sent to an exclusive independent school with arts at the centre of its ethos, and at the age of seven he illustrated a children's book he created with one of his schoolmates. Talk about an overachiever...

Although illustrating a book was an enormous achievement for a seven-year-old, this year proved to be very difficult for him. He was playing in the street with friends when he was hit by a car, leaving him with a broken arm and multiple internal injuries. Months later, his parents divorced, so he and his siblings were sent to live with their father. The next three years were just as tumultuous: his mother was admitted to a psychiatric facility and spent the rest of her life bouncing between institutions. However, this didn't stop Jean-Michel from achieving excellence: by 11 he was fluent in French, Spanish and English. In spite of his cleverness, Jean-Michel struggled with life at home and school. He ran away from home at 15, before being arrested and returning home just a week later. He chose to attend City-As-School, a high school alternative loved by many artists who disliked the rigidity of standard schooling.

Before he was expelled from the school for throwing a pie at the headmaster's face, he joined forces with a classmate named Al Diaz, and the pair started spraying comical slogans on the side of buildings under the name SAMO©. Various media outlets picked up on the satirical street art and began to produce articles and news features all about this curious new writing popping up around Manhattan. His artwork soon became inspired by his Haitian and Puerto-Rican roots, of which he was incredibly proud. He started making postcards with a friend of his, and while selling some of them in SoHo he encountered the famous contemporary artist Andy Warhol. This sparked a friendship that would last several years, with the two collaborating on several pieces of work, including *Olympics* (1984), which shows Warhol's love of colour and Jean-Michel's references to his heritage.

Jean-Michel struggled to cope with his new-found fame and the death of Andy Warhol. He became addicted to drugs and tragically passed away a few years later. Though his life was difficult, his whimsical, sporadic and haunting artwork is still adored and remains the source of inspiration for millions of aspiring artists of colour.

AMAZING FACTS AND ACHIEVEMENTS

➔ In 1981, Jean-Michel sold his first painting to Blondie's Debbie Harry for a mere $200 and was later invited to appear in one of their music videos as a DJ. In 2017, one of his pieces sold for $110,487,500. Lucky Debbie Harry!

➔ When he was 22, Jean-Michel became the youngest artist to represent America in a large-scale international contemporary art exhibition.

➔ Jean-Michel was also a talented musician and was a member of rock band Gray.

➔ The Royal Shakespeare Company's 2016 production of *Hamlet*, which featured a primarily Black cast, contained costumes and set designs all heavily inspired by the art of Jean-Michel.

➔ In 2017, Urban Decay released a nine-piece collection of make-up inspired by Basquiat's work. Coach and Dr. Martens have also featured Jean-Michel's art on their products.

"I AM NOT A BLACK ARTIST, I AM AN ARTIST."

JIMI HENDRIX

27/11/1942—18/09/1970

HIS SUPERPOWERS:

The original guitar hero, Jimi Hendrix created an entire new genre of rock in his lifetime.

HIS INCREDIBLE STORY

James "Jimi" Hendrix was born in Seattle to Lucille and Al Hendrix. Al was a soldier and was denied leave to see his newborn son, so he didn't meet Jimi until he was three. Jimi was a shy child, his timid nature fuelled by his parents' alcohol-induced fighting: he would hide in cupboards to escape the noise. Al and Lucille also had four other children who were put into foster care. One of them in particular, Leon, was always close with Jimi, despite bouncing in and out of the care system. Al and Lucille divorced when Jimi was nine, and his father took custody of him and Leon.

When he was little, Jimi became *obsessed* with his broom. He would pretend it was a guitar as his father couldn't afford to buy him a real one. One of the school cleaners noticed that he carried it like other kids carried teddies, so they wrote to the school asking for funding to get Jimi a guitar, telling them his future would be impacted if it didn't happen – the school declined.

However, when he was helping his dad at work he stumbled across a one-stringed ukulele. He took it home and taught himself all sorts of songs, channelling his love of rock and roll through his one-string rendition of "Hound Dog".

Shortly after this, his mother passed away. Al didn't take Leon and Jimi to the funeral; instead, he gave them a glass of whiskey and told them to deal with their grief "like men". Toxic masculinity, ruining childhoods since 1958.

That same year, Jimi paid just $5 for his first guitar which he played for hours, imagining he was B. B. King. He joined his first band, The Velvetones and his dad treated him to an electric guitar.

Although being a musician didn't pay well, Jimi made it work. He spent years taking poorly paid gigs in the background of major recordings, until 1966, when he met Chas Chandler, bass player of British band The Animals, and the man who would offer him his first management contract. Chas convinced Jimi to move to London, where he would make friends with all the crème de la crème of the British rock scene. The next year, he released his first single, "Hey Joe", which absolutely tore through the UK! He released "Purple Haze" soon afterwards, and in 1967 he recorded his first album, with his second coming out that same year.

By 1969, he was the highest-paid rock musician in the world. Like many, he had a love-hate relationship with fame and found himself mirroring his parents by using drugs and alcohol to mask his troubles. He passed away in 1970. Over half a century later, his death is still a mystery. However, one thing is for certain: Jimi Hendrix remains an absolute legend.

AMAZING FACTS AND ACHIEVEMENTS

➔ Jimi was known for his crazy stage tricks: he would play with the guitar behind his back, with his teeth and he even set it on fire! Don't try that last one at home...

➔ The Fender Stratocaster guitar he played at Woodstock festival in 1969 sold for £1.6m in the 1990s.

➔ Jimi got fired by his bandmates backstage in the middle of his first ever gig because he was showing off. Jimi Hendrix showing off? Never...

➔ When Jimi moved to London, Chas set up the "Jimi Hendrix Experience" for him, a tour in which he could be unashamedly Jimi without fear of being fired by his bandmates!

➔ While in the army, Jimi couldn't cope without his guitar. Even though he got badly bullied for it at the time, he begged his father to send him his guitar in the post. That's dedication!

"WHEN THE POWER OF LOVE OVERCOMES THE LOVE OF POWER, THE WORLD WILL KNOW PEACE."

JOE QUESADA

12/01/1962—PRESENT

HIS SUPERPOWERS:

Marvel comic book artist and one of their chief editors, Joe Quesada is the superhero you might not have heard of... yet!

HIS INCREDIBLE STORY

Joe Quesada was the son of Cuban parents and was born and raised in Queens. From a very young age he found himself enthralled by comic books and *The Amazing Spider-Man* really resonated with him. He started reading the series in 1971, around which time the Department of Health, Education and Welfare asked Stan Lee to create a storyline all about the dangers of using drugs. Naturally, Joe's father approved of the anti-drugs plot, but he wasn't the only one who loved it... The story was set in Queens, so Joe was able to relate to it; but Spider-Man also had a penchant for art, and so did nine-year-old Joe.

Let's whizz through the next few years... it's now 1984, and Joe, having followed his artistic talent all the way to college, has graduated from the School of Visual Arts. By this time, Joe was 22 and convinced that he'd grown out of comics. How wrong he was!

One of Joe's friends had heard he was an artist and thought he'd appreciate the fantastic work of Frank Miller in the Batman comic, *The Dark Knight Returns*. Sure enough, this reignited his old love of comics, and Joe returned to illustration, inspired heavily by Japanese manga.

Just five years later, he found himself in an interview with DC comics, writing one Superman comic, one X-Men comic and drawing one illustration of two regular people drinking coffee. They were seriously impressed by his innovative work and offered him the job. Soon after this, he was able to set up his own publishing company with fellow artist and friend Jimmy Palmiotti, called Event Comics.

Four years later, Joe signed a contract with Marvel Comics to create and edit the Marvel Knights imprint. The characters he worked on were, at the time, considered quite low profile, but just two decades later, Daredevil and Blank Panther are staples in Marvel's ever-growing comic-book universe.

Joe's career blossomed when, just two years after joining Marvel Comics, he was promoted to editor-in-chief. His goal was for everybody to enjoy stories of superheroes just as much as he did, rather than being for a select, cult-like group of fans. However, more readers meant more criticism, and Joe's new wave of comic-book enthusiasts were quick to take issue with one of his 2010 issues of *Captain America*. A plot about Falcon, a Black superhero, refusing to attend a Boston-esque Tea Party protest because he was convinced that a mob of "angry white folks" wouldn't want him there, proved controversial among comic fans. Joe kept his cool and removed the provocative storyline. But he was clearly doing something right, because soon after this happened, Joe was promoted to chief creative officer. Go on, Joe! Keep creating the stories we love!

AMAZING FACTS AND ACHIEVEMENTS

→ When working as Marvel's editor-in-chief, Joe created a new rule that prevented Marvel comic-writers from killing off and resurrecting superheroes too often out of fear that the stories were all becoming too predictable! We love them either way.

→ When he and Jimmy Palmiotti founded Event Comics, they created the brand-new character Ash, a fireman-cum-superhero.

→ Joe has created two DC covers, five DC comics, 16 Marvel comics and 29 Marvel covers so far, and there are sure to be more!

→ In 1993, he won the Diamond Gem Award for the Best Cover for his artwork on *X-O Manowar*.

→ Joe starts his comic-book drawings with really tiny sketches to keep them accurate and then prints them out at full size when they're perfect.

"DON'T BE AFRAID OF FAILURE... THERE'S ALWAYS A LESSON AT THE END OF IT."

KALPANA CHAWLA

17/03/1962—01/02/2003

HER SUPERPOWERS:

When someone's name translates to "imagination", you know they're going to do great things – meet Kalpana Chawla, the first Indian-American woman to go to space.

HER INCREDIBLE STORY

Kalpana was the daughter of Banarsi Chawla, a salesman from Pakistan who earned a living by selling toffee, soap and fabric. He had to support both his own household and the relatives of his wife, Sanjyothi, which was 16 people in total! The pair had four children before giving birth to Kalpana. Banarsi encouraged her to work hard, and when he gave up his job as a businessman to become a self-taught engineer, Kalpana was inspired to follow suit.

As a kid, she would watch the twinkly stars at night and was fascinated by the planes that looked like shooting stars. Her little town, Karnal, was one of a select few towns in India with a flying club. She would often climb onto the roof of her house and watch the planes soar low over her house, waving to the pilots as they passed. After she convinced her father to take her to the aviation club for her first ever flight, Kalpana knew that flying was all she wanted to do. Then she saw a picture of a Viking lander on Mars and realized that instead of just flying around earth, she could fly around space!

To stop her femininity preceding her, Kalpana chopped off her hair and practically lived in jeans so that she'd be taken seriously while trying to chase her dreams. She didn't require much persuasion from her teachers to continue her studies after school and applied to Dyal Singh College to enrol on their pre-engineering course. Naturally, Kalpana passed with flying colours and secured a place at Punjab Engineering College.

Banarsi had missed all of Kalpana's feats because he was busy working, and when he found out about her plans, he was not happy. He didn't want his little girl doing a "man's job" and thought she'd best become a teacher instead. However, Kalpana firmly disagreed, and with her mum and sister's support, she took herself off to college.

In 1982 she moved to America and got an MSc in Aerospace Engineering from the University of Texas at Arlington before getting her second MSc and a PhD from the University of Colorado Boulder.

She started working at NASA in 1988, and when she became a US citizen in 1991, she applied to become an astronaut. In 1996 she was selected for her first mission, and just a year later she was blasted into space on the space shuttle *Columbia*, which made her the first Indian woman to go to space!

She was selected for her second mission on the same space shuttle in 2003, but following damage to the spacecraft, the vessel was blown apart. Tragically, Kalpana was killed in the disaster, but the story of this headstrong young woman will live on forever.

AMAZING FACTS AND ACHIEVEMENTS

➜ When Kalpana first went to school, the head teacher asked what she was called, but her parents hadn't yet decided. The principal asked which name she'd like, and she announced, "Kalpana!" meaning "imagination".

→ At Punjab Engineering College, she was one of just seven girls, and the only girl to specialize in aeronautical engineering.

→ NASA have named a supercomputer after Kalpana, and she's also had an asteroid, a hill on Mars, India's first weather satellite and even a planetarium in India named after her!

→ There were no dorms for girls at her college and she found the hostels for girls in the local area too distracting to focus on her studies. Instead, she rented a one room flat where she lived alone.

→ On her first space mission, she travelled 10.4 *million* miles, and orbited the earth 252 times! She must have been seriously dizzy.

"THE PATH FROM DREAMS TO SUCCESS DOES EXIST. MAY YOU HAVE THE VISION TO FIND IT, THE COURAGE TO GET ON TO IT, AND THE PERSEVERANCE TO FOLLOW IT. WISHING YOU A GREAT JOURNEY."

KAMALA HARRIS

20/10/1964—PRESENT

HER SUPERPOWERS:

Imagine being the first Black woman to be California's district attorney and then attorney general, the first female vice president and the first vice president of colour? Well, Kamala Harris doesn't have to...

HER INCREDIBLE STORY

A California girl through and through, Kamala is the daughter of Indian biomedical scientist Shyamala and Jamaican economist Donald Harris. Seems like "clever" was in Kamala's genes.

Kamala and her sister, Maya, would often sing at both the local African American church and Hindu temple. It was around this time that she found herself becoming interested in women's rights and democracy – all thanks to her grandfather, a high-ranking Indian civil servant who acted as director of relief measures and refugees for the Zambian government.

When Kamala and Maya were seven, their parents divorced and Shyamala took custody of the girls. They moved into the top floor of a small duplex in Berkeley, although they occasionally visited their father in Palo Alto.

Growing up, Kamala excelled in school, all the way from her French-speaking primary school in California to Westmount High School in Quebec, where she moved at the age of 12. One of Kamala's friends spent her senior year living with the Harris family, having told them that she was abused by her stepfather. Although she was young, this was a turning point for Kamala: she was inspired to dedicate her life to fighting for the protection of women and children.

She went on to attend Howard University, where she studied political science and economics. After graduating in 1986, Kamala studied law at the University of California, Hastings College of the Law, where she was president of the National Black Law Students Association. Is it just me, or is that foreshadowing?

The same year that she was admitted to the California Bar, Kamala became deputy district attorney (DA) in Alameda County. She gained a lot of respect from her peers during this time but chose to accept two other jobs over the next few years on the Unemployment Insurance Appeals Board and California's Medical Assistance Commission. In 1998, she was recruited as assistant DA, and after ten years of serving as the chief of the Career Criminal Division she led the Family and Children's Services Division. There, she was able to represent child abuse and neglect cases.

In 2002, Kamala ran for San Francisco DA, and, despite being the least known of the three candidates, she won with 56 per cent of the vote, making her the first person of colour awarded the role.

Kamala ran for the 2020 Democratic nomination for president. The campaign started well, but her popularity declined rapidly after she defended California's death penalty, and she withdrew from the race.

Just a year later, there were whisperings that Kamala might be joining Joe Biden in his race for presidency against Donald Trump, and, following one of the most turbulent elections in living memory, Joe and Kamala won.

An inspiration to all women of all ages and colours, Kamala Harris has changed the face of America – and she's only just begun.

AMAZING FACTS AND ACHIEVEMENTS

→ Kamala grew up during the time of Berkeley's racial integration programme, known as "busing", and was one of the children who travelled to nursery on desegregated buses.

→ At 13 years old, Kamala held a demonstration outside her apartment complex in Canada to protest the fact that kids couldn't play on the front lawn. The policy was changed, and she and her friends played freely.

→ Not only is she a badass politician, Kamala is also a fantastic author! She has written three books: *The Truths We Hold*, *Superheroes Are Everywhere* and *Smart on Crime*.

→ When she was little, she joined her grandparents in a protest while still in a pram. Her grandfather asked her, "What do you want, Kamala?", and her response was, "FREEDOM". Now *that's* a girl destined for politics...

LANGSTON HUGHES

01/02/1902—22/05/1967

HIS SUPERPOWERS:

Poet, playwright, novelist, columnist, activist and all-round literature legend, it's Langston Hughes!

HIS INCREDIBLE STORY

Langston Hughes was born in Missouri to a family with a complex history. Both of his paternal great-grandfathers were white slave owners, and both were married to enslaved African Americans, while his maternal grandmother was African American, French, English and Native American. She ended up marrying Charles Henry Langston (who was of similar heritage to her), a social activist and educator who helped lead the Ohio Anti-Slavery Society. Together, they had Caroline (or Carrie), who married James Hughes, before having two children.

Shortly after Langston (junior – this could get complicated!) was born, his parents divorced and his father relocated to Mexico. He lived with his grandmother, where he stayed until his early teens, when he moved to Illinois. There, he discovered his lifelong love: poetry.

After a short stint in Ohio, Mexico, and an attempt to complete a degree at Columbia University's School of Mines, Engineering and Chemistry, he ignored his father's distaste for careers in the arts and moved to Pennsylvania, where he received his Bachelor of Arts from Lincoln University. He knew that his heart lay with poetry, and nothing was going to stop him from getting there! He was darn right, too.

Several publishing houses were picking up on Langston's writing, and not just his poetry: he was becoming increasingly well known for his plays, short stories and his equally brilliant non-fiction works. Langston was determined to write about something accessible to *all* Black people living in America. He wanted to create work that would reflect the entire culture, be it music, laughter or suffering, which was almost always directed at the readers themselves.

Despite it being almost impossible for POC to get their work out into the public sphere, Langston's first anthology, *The Weary Blues*, was published in 1926. In it was probably his best-known poem, "The Negro Speaks of Rivers", with themes which centre around pride, suffering and what it means to be Black. Although he was addressing serious issues, Langston was never too serious in how he addressed them. His light-hearted approach to writing is what made him so popular with *all* Americans, not just African Americans.

Although he was primarily a poet, Langston released his first collection of short stories in 1934, with the humorous name *The Ways of White Folks*. In these tales, he used his own experience to tell both comic and tragic stories about how people of different races interact.

He later released two autobiographies and after gaining popularity with a younger audience, he used his time to mentor young, Black writers. What a hero! Truly inspirational, his work seems more relevant than ever today.

AMAZING FACTS AND ACHIEVEMENTS

→ Langston wrote at least 20 plays in his lifetime, two autobiographies, three short story collections, two novels, nine children's books and 16 volumes of poetry!

→ In 1941, Langston founded The Skyloft Players, a Chicago group designed to raise a new generation of African American playwrights who were bound to shed more light on being a Black creative in 20th-century America.

→ Although he got good grades at Columbia, he was heavily racially abused during his time there by both students and teachers.

→ Langston and some of his contemporaries (including Zora Neale Hurston, Countee Cullen and Richard Bruce Nugent) started the magazine, *Fire!! Devoted to Younger Negro Artists.*

"THE ONLY WAY TO GET A THING DONE IS TO START TO DO IT, THEN KEEP ON DOING IT, AND FINALLY YOU'LL FINISH IT.

LAVERNE COX

29/05/1972—PRESENT

HER SUPERPOWERS:

The first openly transgender person to be nominated for an acting award at the Emmys, trans-rights activist and documentary producer Laverne Cox is a total icon.

HER INCREDIBLE STORY

An Alabama girl, Laverne has always been openly proud of the fact she was raised by a single mother and her grandmother. She constitutes half of a pair of identical twins, and her brother played her character, Sophia, pre-transition on *Orange is the New Black*.

Laverne has always been a performer – she had always dreamed of becoming an actress or dancer from her first ballet lesson at the age of eight. It was also around this time that Laverne was first exposed to homophobia. Having realized that she fancied boys instead of girls (unlike her male classmates), she was bullied so badly that, at just 11 years old, Laverne attempted suicide. Thankfully, the copious number of pills that she swallowed weren't lethal, so she awoke the next morning with just a tummy ache.

Laverne battled through the bullying and managed to bag herself a scholarship to Alabama School of Fine Arts, followed by a scholarship to Indiana University. After a transfer to Marymount Manhattan College, she graduated with a Bachelor of Fine Arts in dance.

A BA wasn't the only thing that Laverne was leaving college with; she'd become obsessed with acting after a guest teacher saw her performing. From then on, she was frequently asked to perform in plays in the college drama department.

Until then, Laverne had spent her whole life trapped in a body that wasn't hers, but finally, she was able to begin her medical transition and fully identify as female. During her transition, she would often perform in drag shows because it was the only outlet in which she was able to keep performing.

After a lot of off-off-Broadway performances and too much work "for exposure and experience", everything changed for Laverne. Candis Cayne, a transgender actress, had risen to fame when the first episode of *Dirty Sexy Money* aired. She realized that there *were* opportunities available for people like her. She reacted by sending out postcards saying, "Laverne Cox is the answer to all your acting needs" to almost 500 agents across New York, and got four meetings, one of which was with her now manager, Paul Hilepo. That meeting led to episodes on *Law and Order*, *Bored to Death* and *Orange is the New Black*: the break that would change her entire life.

The role brought the struggles of transgender people to the forefront of the media, as well as proving that being trans should not stop anyone from winning awards usually reserved for cisgender actors. She was also able to give anyone struggling with their gender identity a character to whom they could relate and normalize an issue that we rarely see tackled on screen.

Keep doing what you're doing, girl, because you are SMASHING it.

AMAZING FACTS AND ACHIEVEMENTS

→ Laverne is the first transgender woman ever to have a waxwork figure in Madame Tussauds.

→ A social media queen, Laverne uses her Instagram and Twitter accounts to share empowering messages and promote LGBTQIA+ equality.

→ When she won an Emmy in 2019, Laverne auctioned off a replica of her iconic LGBTQIA+ flag clutch bag to raise money for the Anti-Violence Project.

→ Laverne was named one of *Glamour* magazine's 2014 Women of the Year and also one of The Grio's 100 Most Influential African Americans.

→ She's not just an actor – Laverne is the executive producer of Netflix's new documentary *Disclosure*, which is all about Hollywood's portrayal of trans people in movies.

"I BELIEVE THAT IT IS IMPORTANT TO NAME THE MULTIPLE PARTS OF MY IDENTITY BECAUSE I AM NOT JUST ONE THING, AND NEITHER ARE YOU."

LIN-MANUEL MIRANDA

16/01/1980—PRESENT

HIS SUPERPOWERS:

How does a young New Yorker, son of two Puerto Ricans, grow up to be an actor and composer? But it's not Alexander Hamilton, it's Lin-Manuel Miranda!

HIS INCREDIBLE STORY

A true New Yorker, Lin-Manuel was born to Puerto Rican parents and grew up in the north of Manhattan, along with his older sister, Luz. His father was a Democratic Party consultant and his mother was a psychologist, and the pair absolutely *loved* anything to do with music. They took little Lin-Manuel to see his first musical, *Les Misérables*, when he was seven – an experience that sparked his passion for musical theatre.

It was during his college years that Lin-Manuel wrote the first draft of *In the Heights*, the work that would later become his first Broadway musical. The show, which featured salsa music and freestyle rap, premiered at Wesleyan University in 1999. Just three years after that performance, it was picked up by director Thomas Kail. Lin-Manuel worked with John Buffalo Mailer to revise the music and text, and in 2008, *In the Heights* was a Broadway hit – it's since been turned into a fabulous film!

However, this man was not content with being nominated for a Pulitzer Prize, a whopping 13 Tony Awards, winning four Tonys and then a Grammy. Oh, no. This entire time (well, since 2008), he'd also been working on a hip-hop musical named *Hamilton*: a play all about American Founding Father Alexander Hamilton. Being a particularly talented actor as well as a composer, he starred in the leading role. The rest of the cast were all ethnically diverse – something particularly important to him.

The musical absolutely blew up on Broadway and suddenly, *In the Heights* had been overshadowed: last time he was just nominated, but this time, Lin-Manuel was awarded the Pulitzer Prize for Drama and won 11 Tony Awards!

In addition to his countless musical accolades, Lin-Manuel is a very passionate activist. He met with President Obama to discuss settling Puerto Rico's government-debt burden in 2016, and was heavily involved in financially assisting Puerto Rico after it was hit by Hurricane Maria in 2017. Some of the proceeds raised from *Hamilton* are used to support Graham Windham, a not-for-profit adoption agency founded by Eliza Schuyler Hamilton in 1806 with the aim of helping children who'd grown up in difficult environments.

He's always remembered his upbringing, though, and has tried to support the arts as much as he can. He donated $1 million to renovate the University of Puerto Rico theatre in order for it to be used for a fundraising performance of *Hamilton* with himself in the starring role, and also donated hundreds of thousands of dollars to help improve the Luis A. Ferré Performing Arts Center.

What will he come up with next?

AMAZING FACTS AND ACHIEVEMENTS

➜ Lin-Manuel's first musical was a 20-minute-long school show featuring a "dissected pig rising up for revenge that he had cut up in biology class" – and that's a quote from one of his classmates.

➜ During his wedding, he and his guests treated Lin-Manuel's wife, Vanessa, to an impromptu performance of "To Life" from *Fiddler on the Roof* – the YouTube video of the performance has 6 million views.

➜ He received a special Kennedy Center Honor in 2018 for developing *Hamilton*, a musical that defies all genres.

➜ Heard of Disney's *Moana*? Well, he wrote the smash hit "How Far I'll Go", for which he earned his first Oscar nomination, and several of the film's other songs.

➜ As if all that wasn't enough, Lin-Manuel has also written a book called *Gmorning, Gnight!: Little Pep Talks For Me & You*, a collection of little quotes to get you through the day! What a man.

MALALA YOUSAFZAI

12/07/1997—PRESENT

HER SUPERPOWERS:

By 23, most people are proud to have a few pounds left at the bottom of their overdraft and an empty washing-up bowl, but Malala Yousafzai? She can boast a Nobel Peace Prize, at least five books, an honorary doctorate and a degree from Oxford.

HER INCREDIBLE STORY

Malala was born in Mingora, Pakistan, into a world where girls weren't necessarily pushed to be potential scholars or leaders of the future. Her father is a teacher, education activist and the proud founder of two schools for girls, one of which Malala attended and *loved*.

By the time she was ten, the Taliban was rising to power and taking over Pakistan. Women weren't to leave the house without being accompanied by a man, were banned from working and couldn't vote. It was also made clear that they would not support education for girls: over 400 girls' schools were closed, and those that refused to shut were burned down.

Malala was angry. She wasn't going to let anyone define whether or not she deserved an education, so she disobeyed their rule and stayed at school.

When an opportunity arose for a female student to participate in a BBC project about life under the Taliban, Malala was desperate to be a part of it. Despite her father's initial concerns, he finally allowed her to get involved. So, in 2009, she was asked to write an anonymous blog for the BBC called "Diary of a Pakistani Schoolgirl".

The blog was a huge success, and everyone was talking about the girl who was being refused an education. She started speaking publicly and on television about how gender should have nothing to do with education or work. The Taliban caught wind of Malala's activism on Pakistani TV and they were not happy. It seemed that war between Pakistan and the Taliban was fast approaching, and Malala was forced to seek asylum in a private residence hundreds of miles from her home town.

Malala became known internationally, but that came with a price: the Taliban knew exactly who she was, where she was, and they were set on silencing her. On 9 October 2012, Malala's school bus was stopped by the Taliban and she was shot three times, with one bullet hitting her head. She was airlifted to a local hospital. When the UK heard about the incident, she was flown over to Queen Elizabeth Hospital in Birmingham, UK, for immediate specialist treatment at their new gunshot and head injury unit. Against all odds, Malala survived.

After her recovery, Malala returned to school, this time in Birmingham, and passed through the prestigious Edgbaston High School for Girls as an A-grade student, securing herself a place at Lady Margaret Hall college, Oxford. She graduated with a degree in philosophy, politics and economics in 2020.

At just 23, Malala has accomplished more than what most people do in a lifetime, but the fight isn't over: she will not rest until every single girl worldwide has access to a good quality, free education. What an inspiration.

AMAZING FACTS AND ACHIEVEMENTS

➜ Malala had always dreamed of becoming a doctor, but her father knew she was destined for a future in politics.

➜ The pseudonym she wrote *Diary of a Pakistani Schoolgirl* under was Gul Makai, the name of a heroine from Pakistani folklore.

➜ On her 18th birthday, she inaugurated a school for girls living in refugee camps in Lebanon.

➜ At the age of 17, Malala became the youngest ever recipient of the Nobel Peace Prize, following in the footsteps of Barack Obama, Nelson Mandela and the United Nations.

➜ She has won over 40 other awards for her bravery and activism, including a Grammy and an honorary doctorate from King's College London.

➜ NASA named an asteroid orbiting between Mars and Jupiter after Malala.

"ONE CHILD, ONE TEACHER, ONE BOOK, ONE PEN CAN CHANGE THE WORLD."

MARCUS RASHFORD

31/10/1997—PRESENT

HIS SUPERPOWERS:

Marcus Rashford might not have been able to bring football home in the FIFA World Cup, but he made sure that food was coming home to Britain's hungriest children.

HIS INCREDIBLE STORY

Marcus Rashford was born in Manchester, England, the youngest of five kids to single mum Melanie. Melanie worked several jobs and would often go without food to ensure she could feed her children.

Marcus was always destined for footie greatness: at the age of five he started playing as a goalkeeper before heading off to Manchester United's academy, aged seven. He went on to play in their under-15 squad and seriously impressed the under-19s manager, Nicky Butt. He later scored six goals in just 11 games in the under-18s Premier League, and Butt made him the team's captain.

In 2016, Marcus was asked to play in Manchester United's main squad. When another player got injured before a match against Danish club Midtjylland, Marcus was put in the starting line-up. He scored two goals that match – they then won 5–1. Another two goals and one assist against their rivals, Arsenal, sent Marcus well on his way to signing a massive contract with Man-U for a whopping £20,000 a week. That same year, he was called up to the England squad and scored in the first three minutes of his first international match against Australia. In the seasons that followed, Marcus scored 11 goals, 13 goals, another 13 goals and in his 2019–20 season he scored a gigantic 22 goals – despite struggling with a back injury.

Marcus truly shines off the field, too. At the outbreak of the COVID-19 pandemic, children's free school meals ended and families who'd lost work were suddenly without food. Reminded of his own childhood, Marcus decided to use his influence to ensure no child was left hungry. Partnering with FareShare, he raised enough money to feed 4 million kids around the UK. However, he didn't stop there... In June 2020, he wrote a letter to the government calling for them to end child hunger. After initial resistance, the government extended free school meals for children right through the summer holidays. He created the Child Food Poverty Task Force in September 2020, and shortly after that was appointed Marcus Rashford MBE.

Marcus was racially abused by trolls following a missed penalty in the 2020 Euros final. A mural of his face was vandalized, and his social media pages became swamped with comments of cruel words and hateful messages. However, the mural was restored and the whole country rallied to show their support of Marcus.

He's only just kicking off his marvellous life, so we'll be watching from the sidelines as Marcus continues to change the game for millions of families around the UK. (I know, even I'd give myself a yellow card for those puns...)

AMAZING FACTS AND ACHIEVEMENTS

➜ In 2014, *The Guardian* gave him the title of "best prospect" in the Next Generation 2014.

➜ Marcus actually started training with Manchester City for a week before moving to the Man-U training camp.

➜ In his debut season, he won Jimmy Murphy Young Player of the Year.

➜ Marcus has raised £20 million in donations from supermarkets to fight child hunger, making him the youngest person to be at the top of *The Sunday Times* Giving List – he raised 125 per cent of his entire worth, which is a *lot* of money!

➜ At 11 Marcus became the youngest player to be picked for the Manchester United Schoolboy Scholarship Scheme – usually children have to be at least 12. To push him even further, he was fast-tracked, so he'd be playing with players four years older than him.

"THESE CHILDREN MATTER... AND AS LONG AS THEY DON'T HAVE A VOICE, THEY WILL HAVE MINE."

MARIA TALLCHIEF

24/01/1925—11/04/2013

HER SUPERPOWERS:

It's time for super-duper prima ballerina Maria Tallchief, a Native American icon who refused to be defined by her proud heritage, to take centre stage!

HER INCREDIBLE STORY

Scottish-Irish-born Ruth, a lover of performing arts, and Alexander Tall Chief, an Osage Native American, welcomed baby Elizabeth Marie to their family in 1925. Following in her mother's footsteps (literally), Maria (as she would come to be known) loved music and took ballet lessons with a local teacher at three years old.

When Maria was five and her sister Marjorie was four, a ballet teacher came to their little town in Oklahoma looking for brand new students. The teacher was severely under-qualified and even put little Maria in pointe shoes – something not advised for students below 11!

In 1933, the family moved to LA with the hopes of getting the girls into Hollywood and sent them to renowned teacher Ernest Belcher, who immediately got rid of the pointe shoes.

At 12 years old, Maria began to dance under the direction of Nijinska, a very famous choreographer with a new LA studio. It was around that time that Maria realized ballet was everything to her and that she wanted nothing more than to dance for the rest of her life. She lived and breathed it, throwing every ounce of passion, love and emotion into her movement – and Nijinska saw that. So, she invested a huge amount of time and energy into helping Maria to achieve her goal.

She graduated from Beverly Hills High School in 1942 and her father was against her wish to attend college. She followed his advice and moved to New York in search of work, with one goal: to be America's first Native American prima ballerina.

After reading about Sergei Denham, director of the Ballet Russe de Monte Carlo, Maria was certain that she would dance for him. However, she was turned away at the door by his secretary, who made it clear that he didn't need any more aspiring dancers. Maria left in tears, heartbroken. Later on, however, one of the dancers announced she was leaving to have a child, meaning a permanent slot was open – and Maria took her place.

Throughout this time, Maria remained closely tied to her Osage heritage. She would often speak out against negative stereotypes surrounding Native Americans and was involved with Americans for Indian Opportunity (a cultural competency training programme). She was also a director of the Indian Council Fire Achievement Award.

After several successful years with the Ballet Russe and six months in Paris, Maria joined the renowned New York City Ballet. Working with choreographer George Balanchine, she succeeded in her lifelong goal and became America's first Native American prima ballerina for her role in his *Firebird* – and she absolutely *slayed*.

AMAZING FACTS AND ACHIEVEMENTS

→ Maria wasn't only a ballet star… she was also a fantastic pianist.

→ Within her first two months at Ballet Russe, Marie had starred in seven different ballets as part of the company. I hope she managed to get a couple of foot massages in!

→ One of Maria's directors suggested that she change her name to something more Russian-sounding like Tallchieva, but she refused and kept her name, simply using an adaptation of Marie, instead.

→ When Maria was 15, Nijinska staged three ballets in the Hollywood Bowl. Despite being the teacher's pet, Maria didn't get any of the main parts. She was mortified, but not for long as Nijinska gave her the lead role in the ballet *Chopin Concerto*! Patience is a virtue and all that…

"ABOVE ALL, I WANTED TO BE APPRECIATED AS A PRIMA BALLERINA WHO HAPPENED TO BE A NATIVE AMERICAN, NEVER AS SOMEONE WHO WAS AN AMERICAN INDIAN BALLERINA."

MARTIN LUTHER KING JR

15/01/1929—09/04/1968

HIS SUPERPOWERS:

Martin Luther King Jr had a dream that someday, the world we live in might be free from oppression and division. While we're still working on that, we wouldn't have got this far without Mr MLK himself.

HIS INCREDIBLE STORY

Martin Luther King was born into a middle-class family of pastors in Atlanta. Despite his parents' best efforts to protect their children from racism, MLK grew up in a "Jim Crow" world, where POC were horrendously mistreated. However, he didn't let that stop him: he was awarded two degrees and a PhD by 25, and his life had only just begun.

In 1955, a teenage girl was arrested for refusing to give up her bus seat to a white man in Montgomery, Alabama. A few months later, another true icon for POC, Rosa Parks, did the exact same thing. This was the start of the Montgomery Bus Boycott, a protest against segregated transport, led by MLK. Over a year of protests and one bomb scare from a white supremacist later, the boycott worked, and Montgomery's buses were desegregated.

In 1960, MLK moved back to Atlanta where he joined his father as a pastor at Ebenezer Baptist Church. There, MLK and several other civil rights leaders formed the Southern Christian Leadership Conference, a group who promoted civil rights and organized peaceful protests.

That year, MLK and 33 young people were arrested for protesting against segregation in a department store canteen. MLK was unlawfully placed in Georgia State Prison, Reidsville. The case gained traction across the US. President Dwight D.

Eisenhower refused to get involved; however, King was released due to intervention from Democratic candidate John F. Kennedy. Three years later in Birmingham, Alabama, MLK was imprisoned again for his role in a similar peaceful protest. This time he was sent to Birmingham Jail, where he would write some of his most famous words about the power of peaceful protesting.

Upon leaving jail, MLK joined forces with other civil rights leaders to organize the March on Washington. A quarter of a million people of different races and religions gathered around the Lincoln Memorial demanding equality for all. There, MLK gave his famous "I Have a Dream" speech, where he spoke out against injustice. His speech had a profound impact on the government. Finally, the Civil Rights Act of 1964 was passed – this meant that discrimination and desegregation in public places was effectively made illegal.

Despite this success, people condemned MLK for his cautiousness and gravitated towards more radical leaders who were striving for instant change. It was around then that he seemed to know his end was near: on 3 April 1968, he preached about the promised land. The next day, he was shot while standing on the second-storey balcony of a motel.

MLK proved that power could be peaceful, and that we can transform the world with words. What. A. Man.

AMAZING FACTS AND ACHIEVEMENTS

→ In 1965, MLK led thousands of non-violent protestors on a five-day, 54-mile march from Selma, Alabama, to the capitol in Montgomery in a demonstration over voting rights. Following two more marches, the Voting Rights Act of 1965 was passed, and African Americans were able to vote.

→ On the third Monday in January every year, the US celebrates MLK Jr Day in remembrance of his birthday – the only other Americans to have their birthdays observed as national holidays are former presidents George Washington and Abraham Lincoln.

→ MLK was awarded the Nobel Peace Prize in December 1964.

→ Visiting Gandhi's birthplace in India inspired MLK to use non-violent activism to fight for equality.

→ There are several MLK memorial statues around the world, but the most famous is on the National Mall in Washington, where he gave the "I Have a Dream" speech.

"INJUSTICE ANYWHERE IS A THREAT TO JUSTICE EVERYWHERE."

MARY SEACOLE

23/11/1805—14/05/1881

HER SUPERPOWERS:

After 100 years of being wiped from history and a few more recent attempts to remove her from school curriculums, there's absolutely no erasing majestic Mother Seacole from the hearts of nurses worldwide.

HER INCREDIBLE STORY

Mary Seacole was born in Jamaica in the early 19th century, in a time and place where most Black people were born as slaves. Mary's mother was a Jamaican healer, but as Mary's father was a white British Army officer, she was born a free woman. Growing up, Mary learned how to use traditional Jamaican medicines from her mother and was prone to practising on herself, her dolls and even sick animals.

Mary first travelled to England when she was just 16. She was excited to learn all about traditional Western medicine, which she would use to expand her understanding of Caribbean treatments. Travelling alone was unusual for a woman in the 1800s, and Mary recorded everything in her autobiography, *Wonderful Adventures of Mrs Seacole in Many Lands*. In it, she wrote about her experience of being bullied by boys in London for the colour of her skin, even though she described herself as being "only a little brown" to try to dissuade the nasty bullies from viewing her differently. However, Mary didn't get bogged down: she carried on travelling, visiting Cuba, Haiti and the Bahamas before moving back to Jamaica in 1826 to care for a family friend.

During Jamaica's horrendous outbreak of cholera in 1850, Mary wanted to be of use and play her part. She would often watch the military doctors treat the infection. She took everything she'd learned and travelled to Cruces to be a nurse in a similar cholera epidemic there.

When the Crimean War broke out in October 1853, Mary knew she had to help. She sailed over to London to offer her services as a nurse but was turned away as there was no space for her. Instead, she headed to Crimea, where she established the British Hotel with Thomas Day, a place for feeding and treating soldiers just a couple of miles away from where they were stationed. She would also take food and medicines to soldiers on the battlefield, whether they were British, French, Sardinian or Russian.

Mary dedicated her whole life to looking after other beings, no matter where they were from or whether or not they were even human – she was keen on caring for animals, too! For over 100 years, she was ignored from history because academics considered her nothing more than a witch doctor who ran little shops during the war. Now, finally, we can hear her real story and be inspired by the magnificent Mother Mary Seacole!

AMAZING FACTS AND ACHIEVEMENTS

➔ Mary's mother owned her own boarding house called Blundell House, where many guests were injured soldiers. Mary would help to care for the sick soldiers when she was only 12.

→ After spending a year in England, Mary returned to Jamaica for a while to collect jams and pickles, which she would sell in London to earn money.

→ Upon being told it was a shame she had dark skin, Mary made it clear that her skin tone had absolutely no effect on her incredible work, saying even if she had darker skin, "I should have been just as happy and just as useful, and as much respected by those whose respect I value". Go on, girl!

→ A statue of Mary was unveiled outside St Thomas' Hospital in London in 2016, which is believed to be the first statue in the UK in honour of a Black woman.

"AND THE GRATEFUL WORDS AND SMILE WHICH REWARDED ME FOR BINDING UP A WOUND OR GIVING A COOLING DRINK WAS A PLEASURE WORTH RISKING LIFE FOR AT ANY TIME."

MAYA ANGELOU

4/4/1928—28/05/2014

HER SUPERPOWERS:

We've written her down in history, kept her sassiness, sexiness and "haughtiness", and Maya Angelou continues to rise, rise, rise.

HER INCREDIBLE STORY

Maya was born in St Louis, Missouri. Due to family tensions surrounding their parents' separation when they were very young, Maya and her brother Bailey were sent to live with their grandmother. They lived there for four years before their father turned up unannounced to return them to their mother. At the age of eight, Maya was sexually abused by her mother's boyfriend, Freeman, who was found guilty and jailed for one day before he was released. He was murdered four days later – allegedly by Maya's uncles. Following Freeman's death, Maya became mute, scared that if she spoke, somebody else might die. During those five years, she read, observed and developed an exceptional memory. Nearly five years later, Maya and Bailey returned to their grandmother's home, where a family friend and teacher helped her speak by using poetry.

Maya married a white musician in 1951, despite the taboo around interracial relationships at that time. During their marriage, she learned to sing and dance. The pair divorced three years later, but Maya continued dancing and performing in clubs and even toured around Europe. She released her first album, *Miss Calypso*, in 1957.

A multi-talented queen, Maya moved to New York to focus on her writing. She met several famous faces after joining the Harlem Writers Guild, including Martin Luther King Jr.

After a stint in Egypt, Maya and her son, Guy, moved to Ghana for his studies. She became a feature editor for *The African Review*, a writer at *The Ghanaian Times*, a broadcaster at Radio Ghana and performed at the National Theatre.

In 1965 she befriended Malcolm X, with whom she built the Organization of Afro-American Unity before helping another friend, Martin Luther King Jr, to organize a march. Both men were assassinated shortly after – MLK was killed on her birthday. Maya channelled her grief into words and wrote. Her first autobiography, *I Know Why the Caged Bird Sings*, was, deservedly, a huge success.

In her later years, Maya composed music for films, wrote articles and screenplays, directed and produced documentaries, and she was even nominated for a Tony Award for acting. Although she didn't have a bachelor's, she received over 30 honorary degrees from universities worldwide and accepted a professorship teaching theology and ethics, drama and writing in North Carolina.

Maya Angelou passed away at the age of 86 in the midst of writing a final autobiography. There aren't enough pages in the world to lay down every single one of her accolades – what a life!

AMAZING FACTS AND ACHIEVEMENTS

→ In 2010, Maya donated 340 documents (including drafts of her first autobiography and letters to her editor) to Harlem's Schomburg Center for Research in Black Culture.

→ Maya became Oprah's mentor and close friend after they met in the late 1970s.

→ She was born Marguerite, but changed her name to the nickname her brother gave her when they were little.

→ In 1977, Maya had a supporting role in the TV show *Roots*.

→ Maya read one of her poems at the inauguration of former president Bill Clinton.

→ Maya wrote seven autobiographies!

"YOU MAY NOT CONTROL ALL THE EVENTS THAT HAPPEN TO YOU, BUT YOU CAN DECIDE NOT TO BE REDUCED BY THEM."

MEGHAN MARKLE

09/08/1981—PRESENT

HER SUPERPOWERS:

The woman who's still as fabulous now as she was the day she was born; the woman who's proven anyone can be anything and that the tabloids don't define who you are. It's Meghan Markle.

HER INCREDIBLE STORY

Meghan was born in California to Doria and Thomas Markle, who both worked in television – it seems Meghan was destined to be a star! Although they divorced when she was young, Meghan was close to both of them throughout her childhood.

At the age of 11, Meghan wrote a letter to several influential people (including former First Lady Hillary Clinton) to show her disgust at a sexist cleaning advert which stated that women belong in the kitchen. The advert was changed. Can we just take a moment to appreciate what a queen she's been since day one?

When Meghan was older, she went on to study theatre and international relations at Northwestern University, Illinois. After college, Meghan moved back to LA to pursue her acting career. After a few guest roles in *CSI* and supplementing her income by working as a freelance calligrapher, Meghan's big break arrived in 2011 when she landed the role of Rachel in *Suits*. The show was a huge success and launched Meghan into the limelight and subsequently right into the sights of a certain British prince who was attending the Invictus Games in Toronto.

The tabloids heard about Meghan and Prince Harry's relationship very quickly and almost immediately started spreading vicious rumours and racist remarks about the royal family's first potential Black member. Both Kensington Palace and Prince Harry himself had to make public announcements calling for the media to leave Meghan alone.

Nothing was going to stop these lovebirds; Meghan and Harry were married at Windsor Castle in 2018, making her Meghan, HRH Duchess of Sussex. In 2019, Archie, their first child, was born.

While marrying Prince Charming sounds like every kid's dream, Meghan's new life hasn't been easy. Meghan has struggled with relationships both within her biological family and with her in-laws. Being told exactly how to act, what to wear and even what she could call her children took a huge toll on the duchess. Her entire life was turned upside down, and, after battling severe mental illness, Meghan had had enough. The couple announced that they planned to step down from their roles as senior royals in 2020, following in the footsteps of Harry's mother, Princess Diana. This groundbreaking moment was proof that nobody should have to settle for a life that brings them misery, and Meghan has borne the brunt of the wrath of the British press in order to protect herself and her family.

Meghan suffered a miscarriage a few months later, but thankfully, she recovered and in June 2021 she gave birth to beautiful baby Lilibet. While Meghan has dealt with a lot for someone who, on the surface, is living the dream, she's always been an icon for those of us on the outside. She'll always be our queen!

AMAZING FACTS AND ACHIEVEMENTS

→ Meghan used to have her own lifestyle blog called The Tig, all about food, travel, fashion and beauty – the name is derived from her favourite wine, Tignanello!

→ In 2019, Meghan became patron of animal welfare charity Mayhew and women's employment charity Smart Works. Her Majesty the Queen also passed down two of her Patronages: the National Theatre and The Association of Commonwealth Universities.

→ In 2021, Meghan wrote a children's book inspired by her husband and son called *The Bench*. It started out as a poem that she wrote for Harry on Father's Day. So cute!

→ The veil Meghan wore for her wedding was woven from flowers from all 54 nations in the Commonwealth.

"IF THERE IS A WRONG, IF THERE IS A LACK OF JUSTICE AND THERE IS AN INEQUALITY, THEN SOMEONE NEEDS TO SAY SOMETHING... AND WHY NOT ME?"

NANAIA MAHUTA

21/08/1970—PRESENT

HER SUPERPOWERS:

Being true to your own identity, history and self is the best way to succeed in politics, and for New Zealand's Nanaia Mahuta, it was the only way to succeed.

HER INCREDIBLE STORY

Nanaia was born in Auckland to Eliza and Robert Mahuta. She's one of three, and the niece of a real-life Māori queen! She went to boarding school before heading off to the University of Auckland, where she studied Māori business development and got her bachelor's and master's degrees in social anthropology.

While she undertook part-time work to supplement her studies, Nanaia's first big career move came when she ran against Tuku Morgan for New Zealand's Labour Party in 1996. She was then elected to parliament as one of New Zealand's first list MPs, meaning she was elected from a list rather than from a physical constituency. She became the youngest member of the New Zealand House of Representatives at just 26. Crushed it! Darren Hughes has since taken the crown, but pish posh, Nanaia was there first!

Between 1999 and 2002, Nanaia was an MP for Te Tai Hauāuru, and for the six years following that she was an MP for Tainui. Nanaia's political beliefs are centred around work, tradespeople, future homeowners and small businesses. Her dream was always to build communities, improve social services and improve well-being and opportunities for vulnerable women.

In 2008, she prematurely gave birth to her first child with her husband, William Ormsby, and the baby tragically passed away just an hour after its birth. The couple have three other children together, and William has four from a previous marriage.

Following this traumatic event, Nanaia immersed herself in work. Even through Labour's consecutive losses in the 2008, 2011 and 2014 elections, she was Labour's spokesperson for Māori Affairs, Education, Energy and Conservation. In 2017, when the Māori King switched his support from the Labour Party to the Māori Party, Nanaia felt like giving up. She'd worked so hard, but it seemed as though it was in vain. Little did she know that she was just getting started!

In 2017, Nanaia became a faithful member of New Zealand political rock star Jacinda Ardern's cabinet. Nanaia was associate minister for trade and export growth, the environment and housing portfolios, as well as the portfolios for local government and Māori development.

In the 2020 election, she kept her seat, beating the Māori Party's candidate by a whopping 9,660 votes! Go on, Nanaia! That same year, she was named as the next Minister of Foreign Affairs. This was a huge deal: she wasn't just the first Māori woman with a traditional face tattoo to hold the position, or the first Māori woman, she was the first *woman* to hold the position, full stop.

Nanaia has proven that anyone from any background can be anything they want to be, looking exactly how they want to! YASSS.

AMAZING FACTS AND ACHIEVEMENTS

→ Nanaia is a member of the Waikato-Tainui, Ngāti Maniapoto and Ngāti Manu tribes. Her position in New Zealand politics is allowing her to achieve her dream of collectively helping every single Māori person, as well as every New Zealander.

→ In 2016, Nanaia's daughter convinced her to get a traditional Māori face tattoo (moko kauae) on her chin. With this display of her culture she has shown an entire generation of young indigenous people that their tattoos are to be worn with pride.

→ Nanaia was inspired to participate in politics by Māori women in the Māori Women's Welfare League.

"IT'S A BEAUTIFUL THING – JUST AS IT IS IF YOU'RE TONGAN, TUVALUAN, TOKELAU, SAMOAN, COOK ISLAND – TO WEAR YOUR TRADITIONAL MARKINGS OF YOUR ANCESTORS."

NAOMI OSAKA

16/10/1997—PRESENT

HER SUPERPOWERS:

This icon has served us fashion inspo, political activism, mental well-being advice and top-tier tennis – and although she's already won, Naomi Osaka's game has only just begun.

HER INCREDIBLE STORY

Naomi Osaka was, coincidentally, born in Osaka, Japan, in 1997 to Japanese mother Tamaki and Haitian father Leonard.

When Naomi was three, the family moved from Japan over to Long Island in the US. That same year, her father took her and her sister Mari to their first tennis lesson (despite apprehension about such a time-consuming "hobby" from her mother's side of the family). Little did they know what a success she would later become.

In 2006, the family moved to Florida, where both Naomi and Mari were able to practise tennis all day and were homeschooled in the evenings. Naomi didn't compete much at junior level, but she did qualify at the International Tennis Federation Women's Tour on her 14th birthday. When the pair were young, Naomi and Mari would often compete as a team in doubles tournaments. They also played against each other in some competitions. In 2012, she lost to her sister in the semi-final of the International Tennis Federation's $10k tournament.

By 15, she was training at various specialist academies, until she was accepted into the ProWorld Tennis Academy. Over the next year, she began establishing herself as a rising star, representing Japan. By the end of the season, she'd made it into the World Tennis Association's top 250.

In 2015, she won the Rising Stars Invitational four-player tournament, and reached the semi-finals of the WTA Hua Hin Championships.

Over the next couple of years, Naomi worked her way into the top 50, top ten and finally, top five. Not content with this huge feat, Naomi won her first title at the Indian Wells Open in 2017, making her its youngest winner in a decade. After that event, she beat her absolute idol Serena Williams, and in 2018 she beat her again!

While it might seem like everything was going perfectly for Naomi, she's been very candid about her struggles with depression since winning the US Open that year. Posting an open and honest Instagram caption about her mental health issues, she had the courage to show that it really is okay not to be okay, and to point out just how tough modern life can be on our well-being.

Despite her difficulties, Naomi got back into the game in 2019 with a bang, this time taking the spot of number one in the world. In 2021, she had the privilege of lighting the cauldron at the postponed 2020 Olympic Games in her birthplace, Japan.

Naomi is a woman with the world (and a racket) in her hands, and we can't *wait* to see her continue to reign supreme as both a mental health ambassador and a tennis queen!

AMAZING FACTS AND ACHIEVEMENTS

→ Naomi can serve at a whopping 124 miles per hour!

→ In 2020 she was featured on *Time* magazine's The Most Influential People list for her activism surrounding the Black Lives Matter movement and her campaigns for social justice.

→ Naomi has been featured as the main character in a manga series!

→ Naomi is the first Asian tennis player to rank number one worldwide, and the first Japanese tennis star to win a Grand Slam.

→ In 2020, Naomi became the highest paid female athlete *ever*, having earned a huge $37.4 million!

→ Naomi is also a Louis Vuitton ambassador.

→ At the 2020 US Open, Naomi walked on to the court for every game wearing a mask displaying the name of a Black American who'd been killed in recent years.

→ Naomi took her mother's name at birth to make her life as a multiracial child in Japan easier.

→ It supposedly took Naomi 12 years to beat her sister at tennis – good old sibling rivalry!

NELSON MANDELA

18/07/1918—5/12/2013

HIS SUPERPOWERS:

After he was arrested for his efforts to end apartheid, the world called upon South Africa to free Nelson Mandela – and thank goodness they did, or he'd never have been their first Black, democratically elected president!

HIS INCREDIBLE STORY

Nelson was born into the Madiba clan in a tiny village called Mvezo in South Africa, who lived in huts and relied on home-grown crops of beans and maize. When he was 12, Nelson's father passed away, so he was adopted by Chief Jongintaba Dalindyebo. He was thrust into a life of privilege and treated as one of the chief's biological children.

Nelson went on to study at the University of Fort Hare, Africa's answer to Harvard, and the only institution available to POC. He joined the Student Representative Council but resigned when the university refused to meet the students' needs. He was subsequently expelled. When he returned home, his adopted father had arranged a marriage for him. Not ready to be tied down, he ran away to Johannesburg, where he enrolled on the Bachelor of Law course at the University of the Witwatersrand.

In 1942, Nelson joined the African National Congress with plans to "politely" protest against apartheid. However, an ANC Youth League formed, and the members believed that the peaceful methods were outdated. They instead planned to create civil unrest to improve the lives of Black people around South Africa. Nelson remained firmly grounded in his passion for peace.

He spent years peacefully battling against South Africa's racially oppressive government, until in 1956 he and 150 other protesters were arrested and charged with treason. While they were soon released, Nelson realized that the Youth League were right: these protests weren't working. He founded Umkhonto we Sizwe with a friend, a sub-group of ANC members who wanted to fight physically for change in 1961. They organized a three-day strike and for this – and an accusation that he was trying to overthrow the government – he was sentenced to life in prison with ten other ANC leaders. This time, however, he wasn't released.

For years, the world called upon South Africa to "free Nelson Mandela". The government responded with an ultimatum: Nelson could leave if he conceded in his fight for justice. He declined the offer.

In 1990, South Africa's new president Frederik Willem de Klerk arrived and after pressure from the public and his own beliefs, he released Nelson Mandela from his 27-year-long imprisonment. He continued to pressure the government to put an end to apartheid in South Africa, and in 1993, he and President de Klerk were both awarded the Nobel Peace Prize for their work towards this goal.

Just one year later, aged 77, Nelson was sworn in as South Africa's first Black president, with de Klerk as his deputy. He used the country's love of sport – more specifically, rugby – to create unity, and he mended the economy!

What a phenomenal life – thank you, Nelson, for everything.

AMAZING FACTS AND ACHIEVEMENTS

→ Nelson Mandela's birth name, Rolihlahla, means "troublemaker"!

→ Mandela Day is celebrated on 18 July, Nelson's birthday.

→ Nelson co-founded The Elders, a group of the world's most knowledgeable leaders who work to find solutions to complex world issues.

→ Nelson was the first member of his family to attend school.

→ Nelson and his friend, Oliver Tambo, founded a law firm called Mandela and Tambo. In 1991, he became president of the ANC, and Tambo was his national chairperson.

→ Although he retired from politics in 1999, Nelson continued to fundraise for schools, clinics and AIDS charities.

→ Nelson wrote several books, including an autobiography he wrote while in prison, *Long Walk to Freedom*, which inspired the 2013 movie of the same name.

"A WINNER IS A DREAMER WHO NEVER GIVES UP."

OSCAR DE LA RENTA

22/07/1932—20/10/2014

HIS SUPERPOWERS:

With thousands of yards of floral fabric, designer Oscar de la Renta created the most magnificent pattern for empowering women worldwide.

HIS INCREDIBLE STORY

Oscar was born into a hugely cultural family in the Dominican Republic. The only boy out of seven children, he was the son of a Puerto Rican businessman and a Dominican mother who passed away from multiple sclerosis complications when Oscar was just 18.

Oscar moved to Spain that same year to study painting at the Royal Academy of San Fernando. To keep himself financially afloat, he worked as an illustrator for magazines and drew sketches for fashion houses. It was around then that Oscar first realized his true calling: design. The wife of the US Spanish ambassador came across some of his drawings and asked him to design a dress for her daughter. He gladly accepted the challenge, and naturally, he smashed it: the dress appeared on the cover of *Life* magazine shortly after.

Oscar undertook an apprenticeship with Cristóbal Balenciaga (yes, that's Balenciaga of *Balenciaga*), who acted as his mentor. He later moved to Paris, working at couture house Lanvin, but he felt he needed to leave to pursue his own design career. He approached the *Vogue* editor-in-chief, Diana Vreeland, who suggested he speak to Elizabeth Arden. He worked with her for two years before moving over to Jane Derby. Sadly, she passed away in 1965. The label was handed over to Oscar, who accepted it with pride, soon changing the firm's name to Oscar de la Renta Inc. He became loved for his striking silhouettes and stunning silks and was able to share his work with the rich and famous.

While his dresses were undoubtedly beautiful, his goal wasn't just to create gorgeous garments. Oscar wanted to bring the incredible colours, textures and accents of his culture into the forefront of the fashion industry. He also wanted to eradicate the idea that Europe was the home of luxury fashion by bringing a real royal sense of one-on-one, personalized service to the US.

By 2006, Oscar de la Renta had expanded from gorgeous gowns and feminine florals into beautiful bridal wear. His ready-to-wear garments were popularized by those in the upper echelons of society, from actresses to first ladies – he designed dresses for Nancy Reagan, Hillary Clinton and Laura Bush!

However, he didn't want to limit himself to design. He used his creative influence to reach out to plenty of cultural efforts, such as The Americas Society, The Spanish Institute and New Yorkers for Children.

In 2014, Oscar passed away with complications from cancer at the age of 82. Oscar had a hugely successful life, using his confidence and sheer talent to work his way to the absolute top of the fashion world. I have just one word left to say, and that is SLAY.

AMAZING FACTS AND ACHIEVEMENTS

→ After leaving Jane Derby, Oscar worked as the haute couture designer at the House of Balmain, becoming the first Dominican to design at a French couture house.

→ In 2013, he received an honorary degree from Hamilton College.

→ Oscar's Spring 2014 collection was named Designed for a Cure to raise money for the Sylvester Comprehensive Cancer Centre at the University of Miami.

→ Oscar made *Vanity Fair's* International Best Dressed List four times before being granted a place in the list's Hall of Fame in 1973.

→ Oscar was the president of the Council of Fashion Designers of America *twice*, for a total of seven years, and was also awarded the CFDA Lifetime Achievement Award.

"WE LIVE IN AN ERA OF GLOBALIZATION AND THE ERA OF THE WOMAN. NEVER IN THE HISTORY OF THE WORLD HAVE WOMEN BEEN MORE IN CONTROL OF THEIR DESTINY."

ROXANE GAY

15/10/1974—PRESENT

HER SUPERPOWERS:

Even a woman on Insider's list of America's most influential equality-seekers calls herself a "bad feminist", so don't worry: Roxane Gay is here to help us all feel better at trying to be better.

HER INCREDIBLE STORY

Roxane Gay grew up in Nebraska in a middle-class, loving family of Haitian descent, but Roxane's childhood was far from plain sailing. At the age of 12, she was sexually assaulted by her boyfriend and his friends, resulting in trauma which she would take several years to come to terms with. One way Roxane approached healing was through exploring the power of writing.

Roxane began an undergraduate degree at Yale but left at 19 to travel to Arizona – without telling her parents – with a man she'd met online. She was struggling with holding the secret of the trauma she'd lived with for seven years and needed to escape. She finished her undergraduate degree in Vermont, realizing she wanted to be closer to home, before getting a master's degree from the University of Nebraska–Lincoln. To complete the set, she got her PhD in Rhetoric and Technical Communication from Michigan Technological University in 2010. That year, she started teaching at Eastern Illinois University as an English professor, while editing a magazine and founding her own publishing house on the side – as you do.

In 2014, she finished teaching there, around the same time that her debut novel, *An Untamed State*, was released. Her first collection of essays, *Bad Feminist*, was released in the same year, and it's no surprise that it received incredibly high praise. In both the essays and the novel, Roxane explored sex, size, race, politics and sexuality (finding yourself sexy as a plus-sized woman is something she frequently talks about with candid eloquence) – themes that now define Roxane Gay as the amazing author she is. That same year, she moved to Indiana to become a creative writing professor at Purdue University. Given the quality and amount of teaching she was providing, she felt she was paid unfairly, but the university refused to adequately compensate her, so she headed back to Yale to teach instead!

In 2016, Marvel hired Roxane to write a spin-off comic to *Black Panther* called, *World of Wakanda*. The six issues she wrote along with Yona Harvey (another excellent Black writer) were praised for their LGBTQ+ characters, a rare sight in Marvel comics. In 2019, Roxane launched *Gay Magazine*, a magazine about culture, through which she could keep editing but also hire writers and pay them a good wage for the brilliant work they were doing. She later released a pop-up magazine, *Unruly Bodies*, in which she gave a platform to 24 writers living in "unruly bodies" – writers who were plus-sized, disabled or several other things society deems unacceptable – which ran for just one month.

Roxane continues to release brilliant pieces of writing that push boundaries and expand minds, and clearly it's working for her; she has seven awards under her belt and they keep coming! Rock on, Roxane: keep writing and keep winning.

AMAZING FACTS AND ACHIEVEMENTS

➜ Despite her loud literary voice, Roxane has always considered herself incredibly shy – but she's never let her introvert nature get in the way of creating positive change!

➜ When an alt-right journalist received a book deal with Simon & Schuster in 2017, Roxane refused to publish a new book with them, not wanting to be associated with a company who supported people with such vastly different views to her own.

➜ Roxane chairs two book clubs, one for American network, HBO, and another for The Audacity.

➜ Amongst the seven awards she's already won, Roxane was named in *Queerty*'s 50 heroes "leading the nation toward equality, acceptance and dignity for all people". The most wholesome award a person could win!

"I AM NOT TRYING TO SAY I'M RIGHT. I AM JUST TRYING – TRYING TO SUPPORT WHAT I BELIEVE IN, TRYING TO DO SOME GOOD IN THIS WORLD, TRYING TO MAKE SOME NOISE WITH MY WRITING WHILE ALSO BEING MYSELF."

RUBY BRIDGES

8/9/1954—PRESENT

HER SUPERPOWERS:

Most civil rights activists have at least reached double figures before they start changing the world, but Ruby Bridges? She changed the face of education before she'd even turned seven.

HER INCREDIBLE STORY

Ruby Bridges spent the first few years of her life on a farm in Mississippi, the eldest of five children born into a poverty-stricken family. When she was four, Ruby and her family moved to New Orleans in an effort to improve their socio-economic status, where she attended a segregated nursery. One day her class were asked to take a set of tests, and Ruby's life completely changed...

The test was for William Frantz Elementary School (a school for exclusively white children) to find bright Black students with lots of potential, and, being the clever kid she was, Ruby was offered a place. The whole family were concerned for Ruby's safety, as many white people in the area were angry about the attempts to desegregate education. Ruby's mother eventually persuaded them that it was the best thing to do for her daughter's future, so on 14 November 1960, Ruby embarked upon her first day at an otherwise all-white school.

Surrounding the entrance to her new school were crowds of angry people – Ruby thought they must have been gathering for a carnival, but they were there to scream racial slurs at Ruby and her mother. These people didn't want their school desegregated or tarnished by a person of colour. Many parents refused to send their children into school, and things got so out of hand that Ruby was kept in the principal's office for the day for her own safety. She was escorted into school every day by federal marshals for her entire first year. Every single teacher point-blank refused to teach Ruby, all except for one: Mrs Barbara Henry.

Mrs Henry taught Ruby every single day for a year, but there were no other children in the class for the whole time. She had to eat alone and play alone at break time, but Mrs Henry was always there to make sure she was still happy and healthy, like any good teacher should!

Life at home was difficult during that year: Ruby's parents lost their jobs due to the uproar surrounding their daughter, and when their local grocery store started refusing to serve them, it seemed that segregation was worse than ever for the Bridges family. However, many people of all races supported them; their next door neighbour even gave Ruby's father a job!

In her second year at William Frantz, several other Black students joined Ruby and despite a *lot* of resistance, she spent the rest of her education at schools with children of all races, and went on to set up a foundation centred around tolerance, respect and appreciation of all differences.

What an absolute queen, paving the way for future children of colour who'd otherwise be denied an education because of the colour of their skin.

AMAZING FACTS AND ACHIEVEMENTS

➜ Ruby has written two books: one is a children's book called *Ruby Bridges Goes to School: My True Story*, and one is a memoir called *Through My Eyes*.

➜ Artist Norman Rockwell created a piece inspired by Ruby walking to school called *The Problem We All Live With*, which was displayed in the White House's art gallery. The song "Ruby's Shoes" by Lori McKenna is also about Ruby Bridges.

➜ Ruby started working as a parent liaison at William Frantz in 1993, which had by then become a school for ambitious Black children.

➜ Although the main building has since been repurposed as a charter school, there's a statue of Ruby Bridges in the courtyard at William Frantz, and classroom 2306 has been restored to look just like it did when she was a child.

"DON'T FOLLOW THE PATH. GO WHERE THERE IS NO PATH AND BEGIN THE TRAIL. WHEN YOU START A NEW TRAIL EQUIPPED WITH COURAGE, STRENGTH AND CONVICTION, THE ONLY THING THAT CAN STOP YOU IS YOU."

RuPAUL

17/11/1960—PRESENT

HIS SUPERPOWERS:

*The man who has proven that you can always be
yourself, even when your favourite thing is being
somebody else... it's drag queen extraordinaire, RuPaul!*

HIS INCREDIBLE STORY

RuPaul Andre Charles grew up in California with his three sisters and parents, Ernestine, a Louisiana-born Creole woman, and Irving, who was African-American. They divorced when RuPaul was seven, so the children were raised alone by Ernestine. At 15, he and his sister Renetta moved to Atlanta to embark on their careers in the performing arts industry. It was around that time that he started experimenting with women's fashion and first tried cross-dressing.

He applied to appear on *The American Music Show* in 1982 and became a regular on the show in no time. He also formed several short-lived bands with friends. In the mid-1980s, RuPaul headed to New York to further his career as a performer. A drag queen friend called Lady Bunny had started a brand new festival called Wigstock; a place for drag queens to slay on stage. RuPaul gave it a go, and unsurprisingly, he took to it like a true natural. Not only were the audience loving it, but he was quickly recognizing that this was *everything* he'd ever wanted without even knowing. This was a part of RuPaul's whole identity that he'd only just discovered. The festival grew and grew, and by 1989 he was crowned Clubworld's Queen of Manhattan.

RuPaul realized he was bound for success in the club world, so he turned back to his musical roots as a singer for his first album, *Supermodel of the World* in 1993. His song "Supermodel" from the album soared to number two in the *Billboard* Hot Dance Music chart, and the next two singles shot to the top, partially due to their brilliant videos. Now *that's* a queen!

That decade, he also signed a modelling contract with MAC Cosmetics, got his own talk show (*The RuPaul Show*), released an autobiography and then a second album. He spent the next decade starring in several movies and TV shows, including *The Brady Bunch Movie* and *Sister, Sister*. However, this was only the start of his TV career.

In 2009, RuPaul launched his own Emmy Award winning show, *RuPaul's Drag Race*, a reality TV competition and now pop-culture favourite. RuPaul has thrust drag back into the mainstream, and people of all generations have fallen in love with the glitz and the glamour that comes with it. Instead of being an underground world reserved exclusively for the club scene, RuPaul has shown the whole world that drag can be for *anybody*, giving queer people a super safe space to be themselves and just have fun!

He's since hosted a podcast and even a gameshow called *Gay for Play*, and all the while has maintained his musical career. So, it's fair to say that RuPaul has slayed his way through the performing arts world, and six decades in he's just getting better and better.

AMAZING FACTS AND ACHIEVEMENTS

➜ RuPaul was awarded a star on the Hollywood Walk of Fame by one of his biggest inspirations, Jane Fonda.

➜ There's a waxwork of RuPaul in NYC's Madame Tussauds.

➜ As well as co-writing and co-producing the Netflix series *AJ and the Queen*, RuPaul was a star in front of the camera for it, too.

➜ RuPaul was the cover star of *Vanity Fair* in January 2020.

➜ His parents chose the name RuPaul as a nod toward their heritage: roux is the term for the base of gumbo and other creole dishes.

➜ When he was still trying to make a name for himself, a young RuPaul used to sell postcards of his face and little booklets with witty captions and cute messages inside.

"WHEN YOU BECOME THE IMAGE OF YOUR OWN IMAGINATION, IT'S THE MOST POWERFUL THING YOU COULD EVER DO."

SIMONE BILES

14/03/1997—PRESENT

HER SUPERPOWERS:

She's not the next Usain Bolt or Michael Phelps. She's the first Simone Biles, one of the most decorated gymnasts ever, and that's her superpower.

HER INCREDIBLE STORY

Simone Biles is the third of four children born to single mother Shanon. Her mother suffered with substance abuse when the children were young, so Simone and her little sister were raised in Houston by their grandparents, Nellie and Ron – their older siblings were raised by Ron's sister, Harriet.

At six, Simone first realized her love of gymnastics while on a school trip to a gymnasium. She mimicked the athletes, jumping and tumbling so much that the gym trainers contacted her grandparents, suggesting that she enrol in gymnastics lessons. And so it began!

She competed in the 2011 American Classic competition in her home town, Houston. Placing third all-around (meaning she earned the highest score from all of the events combined), she continued to develop her career as an elite athlete before joining the US Junior National Team. Her work ethic for gymnastics was so strong that she chose to be homeschooled in 2012, giving her eight more hours per week in which she could train.

Despite what the press might think, nobody is immune from suffering with mental health issues. In 2013, Simone started struggling with anxiety and low self-esteem. She didn't perform to her usual standard during the US Classic so spoke to a professional about her anxiety, to enable her to unlock her full potential.

She enrolled at UCLA in 2014, planning to start in 2016. But after deciding to go pro in 2015, she forfeited her ability to compete for UCLA at collegiate level. More recently, she has started studying business administration at the online University of the People, where she's also created her own scholarship fund to help students who have been in foster care to cover their assessment fees.

At 16, Simone became the seventh American woman and the first African American to win the world all-around title, and in 2015 she became the first American female gymnast to win 14 World Championship medals and ten gold medals.

She participated in the 2016 Rio Olympic Games, winning four gold medals and one bronze. The next year Simone took some time off, but she was back and ready to compete in the 2020 games – although they were delayed by a year. Despite making several mistakes and consequently suffering a severe lapse in her mental health, she qualified for the all-around final in first place. After a near-fall, she left the competition floor, returning to announce her withdrawal from the US team, and she later withdrew from the whole competition. She still won one Silver and one Bronze, but she was fully aware that she needed to care for and prioritize her mental well-being.

Simone has a future so bright it's blinding, so girl, look after yourself and you'll come back even greater – if that's even possible!

AMAZING FACTS AND ACHIEVEMENTS

➜ Simone Biles competed at the 2018 World Championships having spent the previous night in the emergency room with a kidney stone. She still won the highest scores in the vault, beam and floor events.

➜ Simone participated in the 24th season of *Dancing With the Stars* Despite being favourite to win she was booted the week before the finals.

➜ In 2016 when her medical records were leaked, it was revealed that Simone was taking Ritalin (a drug which increases motor activity, increases muscular endurance and reduces fatigue) to treat her ADHD – and in response to a backlash, she tweeted, quite rightly, that that's nothing to be ashamed of!

➜ Simone helped expose the horrendous sexual abuse carried out by US gymnastics doctor Larry Nassar, which is a huge step in creating amazing change behind the scenes in the gymnastics world.

➜ Simone became the first woman to successfully land the Yurchenko double pike in the GK US Classic. It's usually only performed by men – YOU GO, GIRLIE!

SONIA SOTOMAYOR

25/06/1954—PRESENT

HER SUPERPOWERS:

When a ten-year-old girl from the Bronx who speaks broken English tells you she's going to be a judge, you better believe it, because that's exactly what Sonia Sotomayor did – and then some!

HER INCREDIBLE STORY

Sonia was the eldest of two children born in the Bronx to Puerto-Rican-born Juan and Celina Sotomayor. To give her kids the best academic start she could, Celina bought her children a hugely expensive collection of encyclopaedias, knowing that they might otherwise struggle given their socio-economic status. When Sonia was just nine years old, her father passed away, meaning that she had to teach herself English in order to be able to speak for the whole family. By the age of ten, she'd decided she was going to become a lawyer. She'd been watching *Perry Mason* (think the original *Suits*) and knew right then that she was going to do whatever it took to become a judge.

In 1972, Sonia graduated from Cardinal Spellman High School as valedictorian, having graduated from middle school with the same title. This set her well on her way to Princeton University – on a full scholarship, nonetheless. There were very few female students and even fewer Latinx students, but she still made sure that her voice was heard: Sonia became the co-chair of Acción Puertorriqueña y Amigos, a student organization that aimed to create change for Puerto Rican students.

Straight after graduating *summa cum laude* (the highest praise) from Princeton with a Bachelor of Arts in History, Sonia married a man whom she'd been in love with for many years. However, the honeymoon phase didn't slow her down – Sonia was straight off to Yale Law School on another scholarship! She soon became an editor of the *Yale Law Journal*, was co-chair on the board of a group for minority ethnicities and was semi-finalist in the barristers' union mock trial competition. In her second year, she took a summer internship at a well-respected New York law firm. She graduated with a Doctorate in Law in 1979, and a year later she was admitted to the New York Bar.

For the next five years, Sonia worked as an assistant district attorney in New York before working on intellectual property and copyright litigation in private practice. She made partner in 1988, but when a pair of major senators noticed her there, she was nominated for the role of US District Court judge for the Southern District of New York City. The Senate voted unanimously for her, and she joined as their youngest judge.

In 2009, President Obama announced that he was nominating Sonia for Supreme Court justice, making her the first *ever* Latina US Supreme Court justice! In 2015, she was among the majority in two huge rulings: one being for Obamacare, and the other being the legalization of same-sex marriage in all 50 states.

Sonia proved that anybody can get to the top of the legal ladder with education and *a lot* of hard work. Sonia, we salute you!

AMAZING FACTS AND ACHIEVEMENTS

→ Sonia holds honorary law degrees from Herbert H. Lehman College, Brooklyn Law School and, of course, Princeton.

→ In 1998, she started teaching law at New York University, and then at Columbia Law School in 1999.

→ In 2019, she was given a place in the National Women's Hall of Fame.

→ Sonia's 178-page thesis at Princeton won her the Latin American Studies Thesis Prize.

→ While she moved into private practice in 1984, Sonia was also serving on the board of the New York City Campaign Finance Board, the State of New York Mortgage Agency and the Puerto Rican Legal Defense and Education Fund. Talk about multi-tasking...

"DON'T GIVE UP BECAUSE YOU ARE PARALYSED BY INSECURITY OR OVERWHELMED BY THE ODDS, BECAUSE IN GIVING UP, YOU GIVE UP HOPE."

STORMZY

26/07/1993—PRESENT

HIS SUPERPOWERS:

In his own words, he's "young, Black, fly and handsome", but grime artist Stormzy has taken the world by storm with much more than that.

HIS INCREDIBLE STORY

Michael Ebenazer Kwadjo Omari Owuo Jr was born in Croydon in South London and grew up with his mother, brother and two sisters. He always loved music and started rapping at just 11 years old. Even though he's previously referred to himself as a "very naughty child", he was awarded six A*s, three As and five Bs in his GCSEs. After school he tried his hand at a vocational career, spending two years working at an oil refinery in Southampton, but he knew that it wasn't for him.

In 2011, Michael started freestyling online, garnering a huge following quite quickly, and going by the name Stormzy. Inspired by artists from Skepta to Drake, he started to upload a series of freestyles called "Wicked SkengMan". In 2014, he independently released his first EP, *Dreamers Disease*, and was well and truly thrown into the music industry head first!

That year, he won Best Grime Act at the MOBO Awards and was soon asked to perform one of his songs on *Later... with Jools Holland*, becoming the first unsigned rapper to appear on the show. He came third in BBC Music Introducing's Top 5 on Radio One the following year and soon became the first freestyle rapper to reach the UK Top 40.

Stormzy has always been a huge lover of social media. However, when he was thrown into the limelight it became overwhelming, so he chose to take a year-long break from it. He returned with a bang in February 2017, announcing his return to social media with posters with the hashtag *#GSAP 24.02* plastered across the billboards of London. He released the album *Gang Signs & Prayer* on the date on the posters, and it reached number one in the UK albums chart by the next week.

As well as being an incredible musician, Stormzy has always been invested in political activism. Following the 2017 Grenfell Tower fire, Stormzy performed a freestyle at the Brit Awards in which he spoke out against then Prime Minister Theresa May for her inaction. He also opened the Grenfell charity single – a cover of "Bridge Over Troubled Water" – with a verse about never forgetting or neglecting the victims of the fire. In 2019, Stormzy headlined at Glastonbury wearing a Union Jack stab vest designed by Banksy, which is presumed to be a comment on London's knife crime problem. He also funds the tuition fees and living costs for several Black students during their studies at Cambridge University, under a scheme called the "Stormzy Scholarship".

It must be exhausting being such an absolute icon, but Stormzy is absolutely crushing it! Seriously, Stormzy, you're a king.

AMAZING FACTS AND ACHIEVEMENTS

→ Stormzy has reached number one in the UK Singles Chart four times.

→ He has an imprint in partnership with Penguin Random House called #Merky Books, with his first book, *Rise Up*, released in 2018 – the name #Merky is the same as the name of his charity foundation.

→ Following the death of George Floyd in 2020, Stormzy said he would donate £1 million per year to fight racial injustice for the next decade.

→ In 2018, Stormzy won British Album of the Year and British Male Solo Artist of the Year at the Brit Awards.

→ As a child, Stormzy used to rap in battles against MCs much older than him – of course, he won!

"WHEN I'M GOOD AT SOMETHING, I ALWAYS TRY TO BE THE BEST AT IT AND CLAIM THAT THRONE."

SYLVIA RIVERA

2/7/1951—19/2/2002

HER SUPERPOWERS:

Some people are talkers, and some people are doers... Sylvia Rivera was most certainly the latter, transforming transgender lives everywhere.

146

HER INCREDIBLE STORY

Sylvia was born to a Venezuelan mother and Puerto Rican father in New York, where she was assigned male at birth and given the name Ray. She had a very difficult childhood; her father left the family when Sylvia was very young, and by the time she was three, her mother had died by suicide.

Sylvia was raised by her maternal grandmother, who was in dismay at Ray's "feminine" habits such as wearing make-up and typically feminine clothing. She was consequently abused, so she ran away from home at 11 years old and became involved in sex work around Times Square. A group of drag queens soon took her under their wing. After talking through difficulties in her gender identity, she began identifying as Sylvia, a cross-dressing woman.

In 1963, Sylvia met gay and civil rights activist Marsha P. Johnson, and at 17, she became actively involved in political activism. In 1969, police had raided a Manhattan gay bar, the Stonewall Inn, and Sylvia allegedly threw a Molotov cocktail at the police. In reaction to the Stonewall incident, the Gay Activists Alliance (GAA) was formed by a man named Arthur Evans. Initially, the GAA were solely interested in gay rights and offered no support to the transvestite community.

Sylvia set up the Street Transvestite Action Revolutionaries (STAR) in 1971, with her now good friend, Marsha. The project provided safe living quarters, safe discussion space and an all-round safe place for the newly coined transgender community in New York. Even at 19, Sylvia was a hero!

While she was making giant steps in improving the lives of others, Sylvia was neglecting her own health. She suffered with addiction and her mental health was failing, and she even attempted suicide. Thankfully, Marsha took her to hospital to aid her recovery and advised her to step back from activism and the city for a while.

Sylvia's break lasted around 20 years, and in the time that she was away, Marsha tragically died. This sparked a fire in Sylvia's belly to get back to her reality and keep transforming the lives of marginalized people. She moved back to New York (despite having no home there) and founded Transy House, another home similar to STAR. The gay community had expanded into LGBTQ+, and Sylvia made peace with them, having realized that they'd broadened their views and were now showing respect and appreciation for *all* queer people.

Sylvia passed away from liver cancer in 2002, but her legacy lives on in the Sylvia Rivera Law Project. The organization offers legal aid to low-income transgender people, or transgender POC, which enables everyone to live freely in their own gender identity and self-expression. Without Sylvia, who knows where trans rights might be?

AMAZING FACTS AND ACHIEVEMENTS

➜ Sylvia stood up for trans rights vocally at the 1973 New York Gay Pride parade – for which she was booed off the stage.

➜ In 2007, a musical all about Sylvia's life premiered in New York, called *Sylvia So Far*.

➜ A road in Greenwich Village (just a couple of blocks from the Stonewall Inn) has been renamed "Sylvia Rivera Way".

➜ Sylvia is widely remembered as a founding member of the Gay Liberation Front.

➜ A portrait of Sylvia hangs in Washington DC's National Portrait Gallery – the first painting of a transgender activist to be exhibited there.

➜ In 2021, a monument of Sylvia and Marsha was unveiled in New York – it's supposedly the first monument in memory of transgender people.

"WE HAVE TO DO IT BECAUSE WE CAN NO LONGER STAY INVISIBLE. WE SHOULD NOT BE ASHAMED OF WHO WE ARE. WE HAVE TO SHOW THE WORLD THAT WE ARE NUMEROUS."

TRIVENI ACHARYA

1/12/1969—PRESENT

HER SUPERPOWERS:

Triveni Acharya has already saved thousands of girls from the clutches of human traffickers, and she's only getting started in her quest to keep women safe.

HER INCREDIBLE STORY

Triveni Acharya is a former journalist and forever activist from India. In 1993, she was embarking upon an assignment in Mumbai, doing research about a new film for a newspaper. She came across Kamathipura, Asia's second largest red light district, and, being a journalist, Triveni became intensely curious.

Having completed her research, she went back to the red light area and wandered down the *badnam gaaliyan* (infamous by-lanes), soon finding herself in a brothel. The girls standing around were wearing near to nothing, and she discovered that they weren't there by choice. Triveni confided in her husband when she returned home, insisting that she needed to help any girl she could. A few years later, one of her husband's employees fell in love with one of the girls in a Kamathipura brothel, so he called upon Triveni and her husband to help him get her out of there.

When Triveni arrived to free that one girl, 13 others came forward begging to go with her. Triveni took every single one of them home. Most of the girls were from Nepal, so she got in touch with an NGO focused on rescuing girls from the sex-trafficking trade, which was based in Nepal. The girls were safe, but Triveni wasn't done.

She spoke to her husband further about her desire to help more young girls get out of brothels, and he agreed that it was something she needed to do. Triveni planned to quit her job as a journalist, but she realized that her contacts in the media world could create vast change if utilized correctly.

Having spent three years funding her own charity to rescue more girls, she upscaled her work: she'd free the girls and then leave them in the care of the Nepal-based NGO. This spun out into the start of something truly life-changing for hundreds of women worldwide, as she co-founded the Rescue Foundation with her husband.

In 2003, Triveni received a charitable donation, but it wasn't financial. She was given a seven-storey building, which was to be used as a physical shelter for rescued women. While they received copious amounts of support like this, Triveni and her husband were also inundated with threats – some more scary than others. Two years later, Triveni's beloved husband died in a car crash – something she was certain was no coincidence. However, she didn't give up; she couldn't give up.

Now, Triveni runs three separate shelters, with a fourth coming soon. They have well over a hundred members of staff and receive government funding to keep themselves running. Triveni is responsible for saving around 300 girls a year from the sex-trafficking trade and giving them a real future without fear or terror. What. A. HERO.

AMAZING FACTS AND ACHIEVEMENTS

→ Triveni won the Civil Courage Prize of The Train Foundation, awarded to someone "who resolutely combats evil", in 2011.

→ Rescue Foundation has rescued 5,000 girls since its formation in 2000.

→ In 2010, the president of Taiwan awarded Triveni the Asia Democracy and Human Rights Award of the Taiwan Foundation for Democracy.

→ Triveni wanted to ensure that all girls coming through Rescue Foundation were given the tools to thrive in the world outside of prostitution, so they go through holistic rehabilitation programmes, counselling, vocational skill training and education, and are provided with legal aid to help fight the accused perpetrators.

→ In 2013, she received the Humanitarian Honouree of the World of Children Award.

"WE HAVE LIT THE TORCH FOR A BETTER TOMORROW, AND WE WILL KEEP IT BURNING."

VINE DELORIA JR

26/03/1933—13/11/2005

HIS SUPERPOWERS:

If we're supposed to give our teachers apples as thanks for our education, then somebody needs to get Vine Deloria Jr a few thousand orchards.

HIS INCREDIBLE STORY

In 1933, South Dakota welcomed baby Vine Deloria Jr near the Oglala Lakota Pine Ridge Indian Reservation. His great-grandfather was the leader of the White Swan Band of the Yankton Sioux tribe, a tribe which the whole family had felt a strong connection with for many years. He was born into a family of theologists and anthropologists, so it was no wonder that Vine would find the world of religion fascinating. In 1958, he graduated from Iowa State University with a general science degree, before leaving education behind to spend two years with the US Marines. He then returned to education with a vengeance, gaining a theology degree from the Lutheran School of Theology before getting a law doctorate from the University of Colorado Law School in 1970.

While he was studying, however, Vine also followed his true passion: making change. In 1964, he became executive director of the National Congress of American Indians (NCAI) – a position he would hold for three years. He transformed the NCAI, fixing their bankruptcy and getting 137 more tribes signed up as members. He described this time as more educational than anything else he'd lived through – for a man with three degrees, that's saying something!

In 1964, Vine moved his focus to teaching. He started working at Western Washington State College but kept up his activism all the while. He advocated for fishing rights of local Native American tribes and worked on the case that led to Judge George Boldt's 1974 ruling that Native Americans had a right to 50 per cent of their fishing harvests for the year.

Vine would spend the next chapter of his life as an author; the first of his books, *Custer Died for Your Sins: An Indian Manifesto*, published in 1969, was about the struggle of Native Americans. The book was a huge success and remains his most famous work to this day. He wrote more than 20 other books and over 200 articles about religion, education and Native American culture. He often found himself at intellectual war with scientists, who didn't like his unorthodox opinions on history and evolution. He battled back, criticizing their closed minds and insistence upon relying on second-hand thought, and compared science to religion regularly – much to the disdain of the scientists.

In the late 20th century, Vine established the first master's programme in American Indian Studies in the USA at the University of Arizona, fulfilling his lifelong dream of educating future generations about Native American history and culture.

Vine continued to teach and write until he passed away in 2005, but the Native American community (and the world!) still feel his presence all these years later. It takes a special person to dedicate their entire life to learning and educating, and Vine was a true gem.

AMAZING FACTS AND ACHIEVEMENTS

→ Vine was awarded a Lifetime Achievement Award from the Native Writers' Circle of the Americas in 1996.

→ Philip J. Deloria follows in his father's footsteps as a well-respected writer and historian.

→ Vine won the 1999 Wordcraft Circle Writer of the Year Award for his essays, *Spirit and Reason*.

→ To add to his trophy collection, Vine won the Wallace Stegner Award from the Center of the American West, received the 2003 American Indian Festival of Words Author Award and was given an honourable mention at the 2002 National Book Festival.

→ In 2018, the National Native American Hall of Fame was formed, and it's no surprise that Vine was posthumously placed in it – he was one of the first 12 members.

"DO CERTAIN SETS OF CIRCUMSTANCES LIE AHEAD OF US WHEREIN WE CHANGE THE WORLD RADICALLY BY THE CHOICES WE MAKE?"

FURTHER READING

BOOKS OF NOTE

Alexandria Ocasio-Cortez: *Pocket AOC Wisdom* by Hardie Grant Books

Frida Kahlo: *Pocket Frida Kahlo Wisdom* by Hardie Grant Books

Iconic Women of Colour: The Amazing True Stories Behind Inspirational Women of Colour by Candi Williams

Maya Angelou: *And Still I Rise* by Maya Angelou

Roxane Gay: *Bad Feminist* by Roxane Gay

Supporting Trans People of Colour by Sabah Choudrey

I Will Not Be Erased by gal-dem

We Have a Dream by Dr Mya-Rose Craig

Believe and Achieve by Edgar Chekera

RuPaul: *Pocket Positivity: RuPaul* by Hardie Grant Books

Be the First by Caroline Flanagan

OTHER MEDIA OF NOTE

black-ish: "The Word" (season 2); "Hope" (season 2); "Mother Nature" (season 4); "Juneteenth" (season 4); "Please, Baby, Please" (season 4)

Barack Obama: "Barack Obama and Marcus Rashford in Conversation" by *The Penguin Podcast*; "President Barack Obama" by *The Michelle Obama Podcast*

Chadwick Boseman: *Ma Rainey's Black Bottom* (2020); *Black Panther* (2018)

Dear White People (2014) – also now a great Netflix series!

Florence Price: "Episode 1: Florence Price" by *Down with the Patri-Bachy Podcast*

Laverne Cox: *Orange is the New Black*: "Lesbian Request Denied" (season 1)

Lin-Manuel Miranda: *Hamilton* (2020)

Martin Luther King Jr: *Selma* (2014)

Meghan Markle: *Archewell Audio* podcast (only on Spotify)

Nelson Mandela: *Mandela: Long Walk to Freedom* (2013)

RuPaul: *RuPaul's Drag Race*

Have you enjoyed this book?
If so, why not write a review on
your favourite website?

If you're interested in finding out more about
our books, find us on Facebook at **Summersdale
Publishers**, on Twitter at **@Summersdale** and
on Instagram at **@summersdalebooks** and
get in touch. We'd love to hear from you!.

Thanks very much for buying
this Summersdale book.

www.summersdale.com